Tales of ZAMBIA

By

Dick Hobson

1996

The Zambia Society Trust — London

Designed by Donald Coutts (Natal Witness)
Cover designed by Michael Beauzec (Natal Witness)
Maps courtesy of Zambia Surveys Dept

The Zambia Society Trust
Zambia Society Trust
Zimco House, 16-28 Tabernacle Street,
London, EC2A 4BN, England.

First edition 1996
Reprinted 2000 (Soft Cover)

ISBN 0 9527092 0 1 (Hard Cover)
ISBN 0 9527092 5 2 (Soft Cover)

Typeset in 12 on 14 point Berkley
Printed by The Natal Witness Printing and Publishing
Company (Pty) Ltd, Pietermaritzburg, Natal, South Africa
8780

Author's Note

Publication of this book has been made possible through the generous support of Barclays Bank of Zambia Ltd, the influence and encouragement of Peter Miller in particular, and the sharp eyes and long memories of several other old friends, especially John Hudson and his wife Gretta, and Gabriel Ellison.

All profits after paying the costs of production will be given to the Zambia Society Trust, a British-registered charity devoted to the relief of poverty and sickness and the advancement of education in Zambia.

My qualification for writing this book is that for the 40 years between 1937 and 1977 I lived in Africa, and for nearly half of them in Zambia. From 1978 to 1992, I worked in the London office of Zambia Consolidated Copper Mines Limited. For over 30 years, I have collected books about Zambia, and I have to the present day maintained a close contact with Zambia as honorary secretary first to the Zambia Society and now to the Zambia Society Trust. Since 1978 I have compiled and distributed Press summaries under the title "News from Zambia."

This book is not a history of Zambia, but a collection of stories about the country, its people, its institutions, its flora and fauna, and its past. It is my tribute to the many happy years that my family and I spent there, and, I hope, the means of giving something back.

DICK HOBSON

PLACE NAMES

The place names in this book are those used at the time of the events described. The following lists the pre- and post-Independence names.

Abercorn	Mbala
Balovale	Zambesi
Belgian Congo	Zaire
Broken Hill	Kabwe
Elisabethville, Namibia	Lubumbashi
Feira	Luangwa
Fort Jameson	Chipata
Fort Rosebery	Mansa
Gwelo	Gweru
Katanga	Shaba
Leopoldville	Kinshasa
Nchanga Consolidated Copper Mines	Zambia Consolidated Copper Mines
Northern Rhodesia	Zambia
Nyasaland	Malawi
Roan Antelope Mine	Luanshya Division
Rhodesian Selection Trust	Zambia Consolidated Copper Mines
Salisbury	Harare
Southern Rhodesia	Zimbabwe
South-West Africa	Namibia
Tanganyika	Tanzania
Wankie	Hwange

Spellings generally follow those given in the *Gazetteer of Geographical Names in the Republic of Zambia* (Ministry of Lands and Mines, Lusaka, 1967).

CONTENTS

ZAMBIA

1

ZAMBIA: THE FIRST TWO MINUTES

*I*magine the scene … It is four minutes to midnight on Friday 23 October 1964. The great crowd of men, women and children who have filled the Independence Stadium seem to be holding their breath, so profound is the silence. The last Governor of Northern Rhodesia, Sir Evelyn Hone, and the first Prime Minister and President Designate of Zambia, Dr. Kenneth David Kaunda, rise from their places of honour in the grandstand. They walk down into the arena, passing between and beyond two tall flagpoles for 15 paces. There they stop and turn to face the grandstand and the Royal Visitor, Princess Alice, the Princess Royal, sister of King George VI.

The military parade, which has just enacted the handing over by the Old Guard of the Northern Rhodesia Regiment to the New Guard of the Zambia Regiment, now presents arms, and a thousand rifles clatter in unison, breaking the silence. For the last time, the massed bands play God Save the Queen. As the last notes die away, all the lights in the stadium are extinguished. In the darkness the Union Jack and the Governor's Standard are lowered from the flagpoles. It is now one minute to midnight. Trumpeters of the First and Second Battalions sound a fanfare. At midnight exactly, a spotlight focusses dramatically on the flag of the Republic of Zambia at the foot of the flagstaff. As it it raised, the bands play the National Anthem of Zambia, and an aircraft of the Zambia Air Force flies overhead in salute. On the hill overlooking the stadium, the Independence Flame is lit. The crowds around the stadium roar their applause at the ending of 73 years of colonialism.

The Prime Minister, now the President, and the Governor, now just Sir Evelyn Hone, return to the grandstand, the two battalions of troops march smartly off, and, as the first two minutes of the first day of Zambia's existence come to an end, fireworks light the night sky. Later that day, President Kaunda, in an address of thanks to the Princess Royal, said this:

"Let us all be proud of Zambia; let us be proud of our achievements and of our ambitions for the future of our country of Zambia; but let us also show that humility towards God and friendship towards others which will assure us of our self-respect, and at the same time assure us of the respect of other nations."

2

THE FLAG, THE ARMS, THE ANTHEM

*T*he flag of Zambia, hoisted for the first time at midnight on 23 October 1964, symbolises the nation's patriotism and the source of its wealth. The field of green depicts the richness of Zambia's land, red represents the struggle for freedom, black the people, and orange Zambia's mineral wealth.

The eagle on the flag is taken from the nation's coat of arms. It first appeared in 1927 as part of a coat of arms designed for Northern Rhodesia by the then Chief Secretary to the Government, Sir Richard Goode – after a committee had failed to agree on any of several submissions – and completed by a heraldic artist in London, G. Kruger Gray. The heraldic description was "Sable six palets wavy Argent on a Chief Azure an Eagle reguardant wings expanded Or holding in the talons a Fish of the Second." In simple English, the arms consisted of a shield in which wavy silver lines represented the Victoria Falls, while in the upper section of the shield, a fish eagle with wings spread and with a fish in its talons flew against a blue background. There was no motto beneath the shield, and no "supporters" at its sides.

When Zambia came to design her own coat of arms, the representation of the Victoria Falls was retained, the eagle appears without the fish, but with a crossed hoe and pick beneath it. The eagle stands for freedom and the ability to rise above problems, the hoe and the pick for farming and mining. At the left and right sides of the shield stand a man and a woman, the man in bush shirt and shorts, the woman in traditional dress: they represent the African family. At their feet are a maize cob, a mine headframe and a zebra, symbolising the country's natural resources. The scroll beneath the shield bear's the nation's motto – "One Zambia, One Nation." Like the flag – and most of the postage stamps since Independence – it was designed and drawn by the Zambian artist Gabriel Ellison with guidance from the Ministerial Consultative Committee for the Independence celebrations chaired by Simon Kapwepwe, then Minister of Home Affairs.

The Zambian national anthem uses the tune "Nkosi Sikelel' Africa" (God Bless Africa), a moving and beautiful hymn whose history is little known even in South Africa, where it was written by Enoch Sontonga, probably in 1897. Sontonga was a Tembu born in the Eastern Cape who moved to Johannesburg when he and it were young. He died in 1904 when he is thought to have been a teacher at a Methodist mission school. An avowed Christian with a fine voice, he wrote many songs, but the book in which they were written was lost after his death. "Nkosi Sikelel' Africa" is thought to have been first sung in public at the wedding of a Shangaan Methodist minister in 1899. It was first recorded in October 1923 in England by the writer Solomon Plaatje.

It was adopted by Tanzania as its national anthem in 1961, and at last, nearly a century after it was written, by the land of its composer's birth. In Zambia there was a competition to provide the words, and the final version is a composite made up from the six winning entries. It was first recorded by the Police Band, with a choir provided by the Youth Council of Zambia. It has four verses, of which only the first and last are used when it is played in public:

> Stand and sing of Zambia, proud and free
> Land of work and joy in unity,
> Victors in the struggle for the right
> We've won freedom's fight
> All one, strong and free …
> Praise be to God
> Praise be, Praise be, Praise be,
> Bless our great nation
> Zambia, Zambia, Zambia.
> Free men we stand
> Under the flag of our land.
> Zambia – praise to thee
> All one, strong and free.

The name "Zambia" came into use on the day when Kenneth Kaunda led his members out of a meeting of the national executive of the African National Congress and into Hut No. 257 in Chilenje township to found a new party. At first they named it "Zambesi African National Congress," but at the suggestion of Simon Kapwepwe, then the party's newly-elected Treasurer-General, they changed it to "Zambia", a name thought to have been coined in 1953 by Arthur Wina, the future Minister of Finance, in a student poem. It was 24 October 1958, six years to the day before Zambia achieved Independence.

3

THE PEOPLE OF ZAMBIA

Zambians belong to the great Bantu group of the people of Africa. The choice of the word Bantu to describe the group was made by the German philologist Wilhelm Bleek, who first used it in 1862, in his Comparative Grammar of South African Languages: "The South African division of the family of Bantu consists of one large middle body, occupying almost the whole known territory between the Tropic of Capricorn and the equator." Bleek, who was born in Berlin in 1827 and died in Cape Town in 1875, was a comparative linguist whose pioneer studies of South African languages earned him the title of "Father of Bantu Philology."

The word Bantu, defined in technical terms, implies a language characterised by a division of the nouns into classes distinguished by the prefixes, the absence of grammatical sex gender, and the existence of "alliterative concords" – the prefix of each noun-class being repeated in some form or another in all the words agreeing with the noun of that class in the sentence. It is rather easier to understand how Bleek arrived at the title "Bantu." He devised it from the noun root "ntu", meaning person, which appears in all Bantu languages, or appears in a similar form, together with the plural prenominal prefix "Ba" so that the word really means nothing more than "people."

Until about 2 000 years ago, the only human inhabitants of what is now Zambia were a few thousand Stone Age people, so called because they made crude tools mainly out of stone. They lived by hunting and by gathering wild fruits, berries and roots. The Bantu who began to arrive among them grew their own crops, kept domestic animals, made iron tools and earthenware pots, and lived in settled villages: to a much greater extent than that of the Stone Age people, the Bantu could control and alter their environment. The Stone Age people were gradually displaced to the marginal land – the swamps and deserts. The last of them in Zambia found sanctuary in parts of the Sesheke district of the Western Province.

Most of the ancestors of all living Zambians are likely to have been part of a second wave of Bantu invaders who began to arrive in the country about 1 500 years ago. The Tonga have almost certainly the longest unbroken cultural tradition in Zambia – over 1 000 years. The Bantu "explosion" of migration, probably from somewhere in the region of present-day Nigeria and the Cameroons, and probably beginning with only a few hundred people driven by who knows what pressure, was the greatest movement of people ever known within the continent of Africa. Over the centuries, the Bantu spread to cover most of Africa south of the Equator. In Zambia, most of the main language groups of today arrived from an ancestral homeland they called Kola, the site of the great Luba empire in what is now Zaire, about 300 years ago.

Much of what we know of the dispersal of the early Bantu invaders is derived from distinctions in the earthenware pottery they made and which patient archaeologists have dug up. In the areas in which various groups eventually settled and populated, distinctions of language and custom as well as pottery began to emerge, and the word "tribe" used to describe them. But, says the historian of Zambia, Andrew Roberts, "tribes are not actual social organisations: rather they are states of mind. The awareness of belonging to a 'tribe' simply reflects social and cultural conditions at a certain point in time … It is thus not very useful to assert, for example, that there are seventy-two (or -three, or -four) tribes in Zambia."

Stories of "tribal" origins are usually myths in which the original experience has been compressed and transformed into moral lessons for today, and like such legends the world over, they are full of fanciful and miraculous events. All the languages spoken in Zambia today can be classified in nine main groups with the exception of Silozi which was introduced in the last century. These nine groups speak 19 principal languages, and these have between them another 27 related languages. Thus while it is true that, separated by long distance, Zambians may not understand each other's language, over very large areas there is mutual comprehension. And though not to everyone's satisfaction, it has been found adequate to carry out broadcasting in English and seven vernaculars.

LAKES AND RIVERS

4

The Indispensable Element

Africa is almost bisected by the Equator, and south of it, where the continent begins to narrow to a point, a vast air mass, hot and dry from the north, descends each year from the upper atmosphere to meet the great stream of cooler maritime air rolling in from the Atlantic and Indian Oceans. Towards the end of each year, the meeting place of these invisible forces is called the Intertropical Convergence Zone, and on it depends our rains … What exile from Africa can ever forget the first sweet sound and smell of heavy raindrops falling on dusty leaves and dry ground?

The great plateau of Central Africa is brown and dry for more than half the year. Then, for five months in a good season, rain falls in great tropical storms. Some of the rainfall flies off the land as vapour, some sinks deep into the earth, some runs off the surface into streams and rivers and lakes; some runs down to the sea. A metre or more of water falls on Zambia in a good season – perhaps twice as much as London receives – but since it tends to be concentrated in storms, much of it is is lost, and often much of the topsoil with it. Too much evaporates in the heat, too much runs off the land, not enough percolates down into the cool depths of the earth to await man's bidding.

The prehistoric migrations of the Bantu followed the courses of the great rivers, and people settled only near them or near springs which ran the whole year round. Where no water was to be seen, there were no men, except, perhaps, the wandering Bushman who, driven into the wilderness by the Bantu, made the first borehole by driving a hollow reed into dry sand, and contrived the first pump by sucking water through it from beneath the surface.

The Bantu concentrated their villages around surface water, leaving untouched great tracts of dry but arable land. The teeming cities and rich farmlands of the future depended on the conservation of water and the movement of it. By the standards of Africa, Zambia's water resources are comparatively rich and varied. The plateau is hundreds of millions of years old; it is generally flat and monotonous, but scored down its length by the chasms and folds of the Great Rift Valley system. The plateau is cooler than the lowlands, so that evaporation is less, and it is high so that water can be harnessed to gravity.

There are rivers which flow swiftly down from the plateau, cutting deep valleys and gorges across it – the Zambesi and the Chambeshi, which becomes the Luapula when it has passed through Lake Bangweulu, the Luvua when it leaves Mweru, and at last the mighty Congo. All the other streams and rivers in Zambia are tributaries to these two transcontinental rivers, and the most important of these tributaries are the Kabompo, the Kafue and the Luangwa.

All over the plateau, the ancient rocks beneath the soil hold up unseen sponges and reservoirs of water called aquifers by geologists; these sponges can be tapped by wells and boreholes – but they must be replenished by conservation. In Africa, it has been said by a distinguished naturalist, the prime task of man is not, as Dean Swift said three centuries ago, to make two blades of grass grow where one grew before so much as to make a stream flow for two days where it flowed for one before.

The first serious survey of Zambia's water resources was carried out by a geologist in the colonial service, Dr. Frank Dixey, in 1938. He called for the expenditure of £135,000 over five years on water investigation and development. The amount, nearly £4,5 million in today's terms, was considered startling by the government of the day, though it was to cover a country the size of France and Spain combined. The money was found, however, from the Colonial Development and Welfare Fund, the predecessor of today's Commonwealth Development Corporation. But war intervened in 1939, and it was not until 1947 that a start was made on a development plan for Northern Rhodesia based on the principle of giving "on a modest scale, the bare essentials of social and economic services which all sections of the community require." Water was one of the bare essentials, and new wells and boreholes and small earth dams opened the way to a new life for people from overcrowded, overworked and eroded land and their soiled and polluted wells and streams. It showed the way to the farming of the future which has the power to enrich both land and people.

In that first Ten-Year Development Plan of 1947, there was provision to improve the recording of rainfall, flood levels and river flows, to find sites for dams and weirs, to define underground water resources, explore the possibilities of irrigation, and this work has continued and expanded ever since. There is still much to be done. Zambia has far longer stretches of big, perennially flowing rivers than either Tanzania to the north or Zimbabwe to the south. It has Kariba and Itezhi-Tezhi, Bangweulu and Mweru and the tip of Tanganyika. Some of the huge potential of Zambia's rivers and lakes has been realised at Kariba and Kafue, harnessing the raw power of water as it runs down from the plateau towards the sea; and there is more to be developed in fishing, tourism and water transport. Out of sight are the vast underground reserves of water which have to be replenished as the demands upon them grow – the prodigious thirst of Zambia's cities, the demands of irrigation to feed their hungry masses.

Conservation in Zambia, it has been said, begins with a contour ridge and ends with Kariba. Without water, there is no life.

5

OUR ONLY PORT

*I*n 1878, John and Frederick Moir, pious and successful Scottish businessmen, founded the Livingstonia Central Africa Company, later to become famous as the African Lakes Corporation, or "Mandala", John Moir's nickname from the reflection of light from his spectacles. The company's capital was subscribed by two other Scotsmen, the shipping magnates James Stevenson and Sir William Kackinnon, who during their lifetimes gave the modern equivalent of some £45 million to African projects. The Moir brothers, like Stevenson and Mackinnon, had been fired by Dr. Livingstone's appeal for "Christianity and commerce" to open up Africa – missionaries to implant Christian ideals, commerce to advance civilisation and self-support.

The highway for commerce into the heart of Livingstone's country lay from the coast of Mozambique, along the Zambesi and the Shire rivers to Lake Nyasa. The Moirs' task, as unpaid volunteers, was to explore a porterage route through the bush to link the north end of Lake Nyasa with the south end of Lake Tanganyika. It was grandly named the Stevenson Road after Mandala's chairman. In May 1890, Mandala established a station at Kituta Bay at the south end of Lake Tanganyika. Three years later, on the plateau above the lake, the British South Africa Company established its most northerly outpost, a stockade named after the Company's president, the Duke of Abercorn.

In July 1914, a month before the First World War broke out, the Germans completed the railway line between Dar es Salaam and Kigoma on the eastern shore of the Lake. After the war, the salvaged German warship Von Gotzen, renamed the Liemba, made regular calls at Kituta, but had to anchor a mile out because of the shallow waters, and goods and passengers came ashore in dugout canoes. In 1925, John Venning, a district officer and pioneer motorist, took his Ford down the bullock-car track from Abercorn to Kituta and got it stuck in the sand. For his fishing trips thereafter, it became a day's walk down and a hard day's walk back up again. He used to camp under a small hill called Mpulungu, and soon realised it was a far better site for a harbour than Kituta – sheltered from the weather and with deep water close inshore.

In 1926, the first Governor of Northern Rhodesia, Sir Hubert Stanley, made an official visit to Abercorn and Venning made sure he saw Mpulungu. Stanley was impressed by the site, but not by its inaccessability. Venning said he could build a motor road for £50 – about £1 500 in today's money. At that time, the Government allowance for road building was 10s a mile and Venning, with considerable experience behind him – he had built the Kawambwa-Fort Rosebery road among others – reckoned his route of about 27 miles from Abercorn could just about be done within the budget. It took three months and proved so satisfactory that all the motorists in Abercorn took to driving down to meet the Liemba whenever it called. Sharpe, the captain, approved of Mpulungu and asked for a 40-foot jetty for loading and unloading. Venning not only built the jetty, but added a Customs warehouse for the £150 he was allowed. Business at the port steadily increased, and a lorry service was soon introduced.

Early in 1995, the operations manager of the Mpulungu Harbour Corporation reported that the port's capacity was to be extended with new handling equipment: although much of the current 7 000 tonnes a month was swollen by food and blankets for Rwandan refugees in Zaire, there was a regular export trade from Zambia, Zimbabwe and Malawi, much of it sugar and cement, and all of it still carried by the old Liemba.

6

NDOLA'S SUNKEN LAKES

*T*here are several small, very deep pools in the Ndola district which have always been called "the sunken lakes." They are found in limestone and were caused by the action of water on the rock, dissolving it and forming caves which eventually collapsed, leaving deep holes filled with water. The most impressive of them is Kashiba, which means "small lake." It is reached via Mpongwe and St Anthony's Mission. It is about 3,5ha in area and about 100m deep. The water level is about 10m below the surrounding forest, and through the clear blue water, fish are easy to

Chilengwa, deepest of Ndola's sunken lakes, source of many tales.

see – mostly bream, with some barbel. But it may still be true today that some people will not eat fish from Kashiba because it used to be said "even if you leave the fish on the fire all day and all night, it will not be cooked."

Kashiba is also said to contain a monster called "Ichitapa" or "Isoka Ikulu." When a man stands on the rocks at the lake's edge, with his shadow over the water, the monster comes up from the depths and catches the shadow, so that the victim becomes paralysed and falls in the water … But the best known of the legends of Kashiba goes back to the earliest history of the Lamba people, to Kabunda, son of Chipimpi, the chief who came from the west with seeds to plant the first gardens for the people. One day, when Chipimpi's people had finished plastering a grain store, he gave them all porridge to eat, but to Kabunda and his nephew he gave a goat so that they might wash off the mud with the goat's blood. But Kabunda demanded the blood of a man, and Kapimpi gave him a slave to kill. Kabunda killed the slave with his hoe, saying: "Now we are the people of the Hair Clan, for we have killed a man with hair on his head. But you, my father and my cousin, are people of the Goat Clan." And Kabunda slew Chipimpi and became chief.

In time, Kabunda began to ill-treat the younger relatives of Chipimpi, members of the Goat Clan, and they became angry, saying they were of the chief's clan and should not be treated thus. "Let us now kill ourselves! Let us see what will remain! Kabunda can remain, and the kingdom can be his!" So they all went to Kashiba, where they took all their goods and chattels, goats and chickens and dogs, and tied themselves together with a long rope and threw themselves into the lake. But a member of the Leopard Clan was at the end of the rope, and at the last moment, he cut it in front of his wife and carried her back to the village, where she became the mother of all the Goat Clan.

Lake Ishiku, close to Ndola, is small and almost circular and about 80m deep. Legend says that long ago the Lamba chiefs punished wrong-doers by weighting them with stones and casting them into the lake. It is also said to be the home of giants, Ifibanda or Ifiwa, who demand presents of white beads and the blood of livestock before fishing can begin. Lake Chilengwa, which is not far away from Lake Ishiku, is sometimes called "Chilengwa na Lesa", or "Made by God," for it has no obvious water sup-ply. Both geology and tradition suggest it may be connected underground to Ishiku. Tradition says it is the home of a great snake, and that the bod-ies of its victims are sometimes found in Ishiku. Chilengwa is the most deeply sunken of the lakes, with almost vertical walls rising 30m above the water, which is about 20m deep.

7

THE KALAMBO FALLS

In the very far north of Zambia, close to the Tanzania border and to Mbala and Lake Tanganyika is one of the most impressive waterfalls in Africa – the Kalambo Falls, a stream of water falling as though from a gigantic tap, falling vertically from a notch in dark, towering cliffs of rock. The height of the falls was first measured in 1913 by an Mbala farmer, Lionel Smith, and the district commissioner, Chris Draper. Smith climbed down the rock face to the bottom of the gorge, and Draper lowered a stone tied to a string which he held out over the gorge on a palm pole. When the stone touched the water, Smith fired a shot from his rifle. They measured the string and found it to be 701 feet long. This was remarkably accurate for such a crude method: later more scientific measurement made it 704 feet (214m).

Smith said the gorge was an eerie place, dark and damp with spray, and in the swirling pool at the foot of the falls a dead wild pig was churning round and round. When he fired his rifle, the sound of the shot echoed from cliff to cliff in the narrow gorge, each echo seconds apart from the next.

In modern times, the name Kalambo is associated with one of the most important archaeological sites in Africa. Just above the Falls, where the waters of the Kalambo river find their way over the edge of the Rift Valley escarpment into Lake

The Kalambo Falls, at 214m recorded by Whitaker's Almanack as the thirteenth highest in the world.

Tanganyika, there is a basin which at one time contained a lake – before the dammed-up waters broke through and drained it. Excavations which began in 1956 have revealed abundant and valuable evidence of Early Stone Age man's occupation of the area, perhaps 100 000 years ago. Not only his stone tools and weapons, but the charred logs, ash and charcoal, preserved in the lowest, waterlogged levels of the basin, are the earliest evidence in sub-Saharan Africa of one of mankind's first great discoveries – the use of fire.

8

LAKE BANGWEULU

*T*he missionary Dan Crawford, who walked into the far interior from Benguella on the west coast in 1889 said that Bangweulu, commonly translated as "Where the water meets the sky" is only the short version of the fisherman's full name for the great lake and its swamps: "Bangweuluwavikilwanshimangomwana" – "the Lake so stormy that it must be propitiated by the voyager and so wide that you must take provisions aboard for a trans-Lake voyage." Bangweulu is Zambia's own lake, not shared with any other country. It is a shallow depression, part of the Rift Valley system, rarely more than 15 to 20 feet deep, and surrounded by flat country so that it is just possible, in a canoe, to get out of sight of land. It does not get the sudden, fierce storms of such lakes as Nyasa, Tanganyika or Kariba, but it can become choppy and dangerous for small boats and canoes. At its greatest length, Bangweulu is about 75km north to south and about 35km from east to west. South and east of the lake is the vast swamp, larger than the lake. During the rains, lake and swamp spread out from some 7 200sq km to about 11 600sq km. Travel in the swamps is through channels, some straight and man-made, others twisting and narrow made by currents. The landscape may be of short reeds with a view for miles, or high papyrus making a green tunnel.

The lake is formed by the Chambeshi River which leaves the lake as the Luapula, and then runs in a huge semi-circle before joining Lake Mweru, which in turn is drained by the Luvua River – which becomes the mighty Congo.

In the First World War, supplies for the troops in East Africa were sent from the railhead at Ndola across the Pedicle to Kapalala and up the Luapula to Nsumbu on Lake Bangweulu. At Nsumbu, convoys of canoes entered the Chambishi and goods and passengers joined the motor road to Kasama at the present road bridge. At its peak in the war, there were 900 canoes on the river, and the water route was used for years afterwards for mail and goods.

The first European to see the great lake and its swamps may have been Dr. Francisco Jose de Lacerda e Almeida, the Portuguese explorer. He landed in Africa two centuries ago with an urgent mission to establish an overland link between Angola and Mozambique before the British advanced any further from the Cape, which they had occupied a few years before. Whether or not he passed by Bangweulu will never be known. He set out from Sena in 1797, but suffered almost continuous fever and died, it is thought, at or near Kazembe's village south of Lake Mweru on 18 October 1798. We know that David Livingstone first saw the Lake on 18 July 1868, five years before his death in those same swamps, in fatal pursuit of the belief that Bangweulu would prove to be the source of the Nile. It is a version of his name for it (Bangweolo) that is still used.

The people of the lake, the Unga and the Batwa, are expert fishermen and makers of canoes from small, one-man dugouts to giants made from the wood of the mofu tree; the earliest records speak of their trade in dried fish, nets, mats and baskets which they exchanged for hoes, axes and spearheads. They have a legend that a great monster, Chipekwe, lives in the deepest part of the lake, and those who are forced to cross there do so in silence for fear of disturbing the beast, which has a smooth, dark body and a single ivory horn. At certain times of the year, it drives all the fish into the swamps and deprives the fishermen of their prey. The legend was taken seriously in the early days. Carl Hagenbeck, a famous German trainer and dealer in wild animals, believed it to have been depicted in Bushman cave paintings, and actually sent an expedition to capture one on the Luapula, but they were driven back by fever. Hector Croad, a pioneer magistrate, heard a "tremendous splashing" near a deep lake one night, and found a strange spoor on the bank next morning. And the son of the Paramount Chief of the Aushi, said his grandfather could remember the killing of one in the Luapula ... Over 60 species of fish have been identified in the region – from tiny creatures to the huge, predatory Lombolombo (Cornish Jack) which gobbles them up. The marshes are famous as the only home of the black lechwe, and for sitatunga, while tsessebe love the short grass of the open flats; and there are oribi and eland, zebra, hartebeest and roan as well as the lion and leopard which prey on them. The Bangweulu region is noted too for its bird life – game birds and song birds, brilliant birds – and the shoebill, of which a tale is told elsewhere. Nearly half a century ago, it was said of Bangweulu that "in fair weather or foul, the attraction of the lake remains unaltered, a delight to eyes wearied by an abundance of trees, its cool breezes a pleasant change from the dust of the road ..."

9

MUSI-O-TUNYA

*L*ong ago, the Tonga people around what is now Livingstone used to call the Victoria Falls "Shungu na Mutitima," very like "Musi-o-Tunya", "the Smoke that Rises" (though according to Fwanyanga Mulikita, they qualified it with "mufuba wati nkayoke mulilo" (a fool might think he could collect fire from it.")

But the Tonga name has long since been replaced by the one given to the Falls by the Kololo people who invaded western Zambia from the south 150 years ago. It is said that their chief, Sebituane, himself gave the great waterfall the name which David Livingstone misspelt as "Mosi-oa-Tunya" and mistranslated as "The Smoke that Thunders."

Livingstone first saw the Falls on 17 November 1855, but at that time gave them only a brief and matter-of-fact description in his diary, guessing them to have half their real breadth and height. It was his publisher, John Murray, who inspired such later phrases as "scenes so lovely must have been gazed upon by angels in their flight," and Livingstone himself realised that though the Falls were of no practical value to him, they might draw the attention of the British public to the scenes of his exploration, especially if they were named after Queen Victoria, "the only English name I have affixed to any part of the country." Over the next two days he planted peach and apricot stones and coffee seeds on what he christened Garden Island – but now called Livingstone Island – near the brink, made better measurements, and carved his initials on a tree on the island – the only occasion on which he "indulged in this piece of vanity."

The Victoria Falls are 1 708m wide and 103m high. It is the largest curtain of falling water known anywhere in the world. When the Zambesi is at its lowest, about November or December, some 20 000 cubic metres of water flow over the lip of the Falls each minute, and the dark eroded rock is revealed. By March or April, the rains have filled the hundreds of streams which feed the river, and the flow is up to 30 times greater: 550 000 cubic metres a minute pour into the chasm below. At this time, almost everything is hidden by the spray which rises high in the air, making it visible 30km away to travellers on the road from Lusaka. The hydro-electric potential of the Zambesi at the Falls was realised as early as 1901 by the African Concessions Company which obtained water power rights for 75 years. But nothing came of it until 1934, when the Victoria Falls & Transvaal Power Co. undertook to build a 1 000 kilowatt generator for the Livingstone Municipality. The power station was built at the Silent Pool in the Third Gorge, and the first turbine was set in motion on 16 March 1938.

The dark rock of the Falls and its zig-zag of gorges is basalt, formed from great sheets of molten lava which spread out long before the Zambesi existed, perhaps 150 million years ago. The basalt is broken by vertical cracks filled with softer material which the tremendous power of the river seeks out and destroys: from time to time, blocks of the basalt itself break away. The northern lips of at least seven transverse gorges were once full-scale Victoria Falls, and in geological terms, the Falls are quite recent. Only 30 000 years ago they were about 8km downstream of their present position. In time, they will cut back a further 3km to the point at which the Zambesi takes a great bend to the south, and upstream from here, the Falls will gradually change into a series of rapids. Eventually, there will be only a gradually deepening gorge through which the river will run quite peacefully.

The next "fall-line" of the Falls may well be at its westernmost part, the Devil's Cataract, where its bed is lower and much of the flow concentrates. To the east is the 830m wide Main Falls, divided by Livingstone Island from the Rainbow Falls, easily seen from the promontory on the Zambian side which is joined to the mainland by the Knife Edge footbridge. It is here that rainbows, often double, are most frequently seen in the spray, bringing beauty as well as awe to the watcher of this most dramatic of natural spectacles.

Musi-o-Tunya, the Victoria Falls, showing the Knife-Edge footbridge.

10
GETTING OUT OF THE WATER

The valley of the Upper Zambesi is a diamond-shaped plain, almost treeless and therefore free of the tsetse fly that kill cattle. It is a land of lush grazing, and at about 150km long and 50km wide, it is one of the most extensive in Central Africa. To the people who lived there long ago, it was the centre of their world, and they called it Bulozi, the land of the Lozi. The most important event in the Lozi people's lives was the flooding of the plain each year between February and July. In March, the month the people called Liatamanyi, the month of much water, the floodplain is like an ocean. "As the traveller enters the plain and the ragged edge of the forest tree-line recedes, the mazulu – conspicuous and sometimes huge mounds – scattered over it ... appear like galleons frozen in motion," writes the historian Gwyn Prins. "The trees which shade each village are sails, dark and leafy against the bright, grassy sea of the plain ..." Some of the mazulu were made by man alone, but most probably began as termite mounds to which men added their labours.

Today, most of the people live on the mukulo, the margins of the flood plain to which in olden times the people migrated and built temporary villages when the waters rose. This move was called Ku omboka, to get out of the water, and it is still performed each year as the most colourful ceremony in Zambia, filled with elaborate ceremonies of dancing, singing and feasting, a symbolic demonstration that the Litunga is the Lord of the Earth, and of the flood, and of men. About April, when the moon is full and the omens are propitious, the ceremony begins with a member of the royal family – sometimes the great Lozi chief, the Litunga himself – striking the royal drums to summon the indunas who paddle the great barge. On the morning of Ku omboka, the mutango, a drum beaten on every night of the Litunga's life, calls the common people to the dry weather capital of Lealui. When the Litunga has given permission, and led by the royal barge, the Nalikwanda, the people move in a swarm of canoes from Lealui to the wet weather palace at Limulunga.

The design of the Nalikwanda is unchanged since the early 19th century, when a new vessel was usually built each year. The cutting of new wood, its transport to the capital, the shaping and building, adornment, launching and first voyage were an expression and symbol of the people's unity. It is a boat some 30m long by 4m wide, built of planks bound together with the roots of the mukenge tree. Amidships is the lutanga, a hive-shaped cabin covered with white cloth in which the king sits on a throne. In 1892, the great chief Lewanika ordered a huge Nalikwanda, some 40m in length, but it was too big, and it failed. The present Nalikwanda is paddled by about 60 men down the canal linking Limulunga with the Zambesi – dug, at Lewanika's order, to link his palace with the river: it took the labour of thousands to complete.

Today the Ku omboka is Zambia's best-known ceremony and an international tourist attraction. But in Bulozi it is much more than that. It is a royal ritual filled with meaning and with the people's history.

The Nalikwanda, state barge of the Litunga, used in the annual ceremony of Ku omboka. This picture shows the arrival of the Nalikwanda at the wet weather palace of Limulunga on 15 March 1962.

11
WHERE THE RIVERS MEET

The Portuguese were the first whites to explore the Zambesi river from its mouth in the Indian Ocean. Their settlement at Sena, near the confluence of the the Shire with the Zambesi, was founded about 1530. By 1560, a small number of Portuguese were living at Tete, and there is an unconfirmed report of a settlement at Zumbo, where the Luangwa meets the Zambesi, from 1546 to 1600, when it was abandoned. It is much more certain that about 1725, a group of Portuguese moved from an island in the Zambesi, Chitakatira, which had become overcrowded, to Zumbo, to continue the trade in gold, ivory and copper which they had developed with Katanga and the basin of the Kafue river.

In pursuit of this trade, they established a market across the

Where the rivers meet: the confluence of the Luangwa with the Zambesi and the meeting place of Zambia, Zimbabwe and Mozambique.

Luangwa. The Portuguese word for "market" is "feira", and for two and a half centuries thereafter, the township now called Luangwa was named Feira. For 30 years, Fr. Pedro da Santissima Trindade was Vicar of Zumbo, a post he held with distinction: indeed, his medical skills were still remembered when Livingstone passed down the Zambesi a century later. He died in 1751. By 1763, Zumbo had a community of 200 families and was raised to the status of a township – causing some resentment in Feira which considered itself more important, though its population was smaller.

By 1798, when the Portuguese explorer De Lacerda was seeking an overland route between Mozambique and Angola, Feira and Zumbo were largely ignored, and the main trade route ran from Tete, across the middle reaches of the Luangwa, and around the north end of Lake Bangweulu. It seems that in 1804, Zumbo was attacked by Chief Mburuma's people and that the refugees crossed to Feira where they built a new settlement protected by a stone wall. This proved inadequate against a further attack in 1813 in which Feira was almost destroyed by fire. It was rebuilt, but when Zumbo was again attacked in 1836, both it and Feira were abandoned, and when Livingstone passed by in 1856, he found only ruins. Amid the rubble that had been the church, he found fragments of its big bronze bell: one of them is in the Livingstone Museum.

The first boma was opened at Feira by the British South Africa Company in 1901. Low-lying (300m above sea level) and hot, it was nevertheless an important staging and customs post on the route from south-west to north-east. Goods came up by barge from Tete and from Feira up the Luangwa to its confluence with the Lunsemfwa at the old boma of Fundu, and up the Zambesi to a point near the confluence with the Kafue. Many thousands of recruits passed through Feira on their way to work on farms in the south. The Luangwa Valley was almost free of tsetse fly in those days, and huge numbers of cattle came down from as far north as Tanganyika to replenish the Southern Rhodesian herds destroyed by the rinderpest epidemic of 1896, a fearful plague which over vast areas almost exterminated both cattle and wild game. The new herds were swum across the Zambesi – at the cost of feeding a few to the crocodiles – at a point 10km up river. For the hardy drovers who led these long treks, Feira became a popular resting place, and from 1904 to 1916 it boasted two hotels (one with a billiard room) and a bar. But tsetse fly had moved into the Valley by 1915, and with the ending of the cattle treks, the hotels closed, and Feira began to fade away. In 1925, the Governor, Sir Herbert Stanley, ordered a survey of a direct route to the Eastern Province, and the beginnings of the Great East Road finally ended the importance of Feira.

12

KARIBA

*U*ntil the second day of December 1958, the Zambesi river followed its ageless, peaceful course through an alluvial plain until it suddenly plunged into a deep gorge formed by the convergence of two ranges of hills. For 26km, the river ran fast and treacherous. This was the Kariba Gorge, a century ago considered only as a serious obstacle to navigation. It was not until 1912 that a district commissioner visiting from Southern Rhodesia became the first man to report the potential of the gorge as the site of a dam to irrigate the Zambesi Valley – but there was no money for it. In 1922, it was suggested as a source of hydro-electric power – but again there was no money for it. But by 1937, it was becoming clear that the development of the Copperbelt in Northern Rhodesia and of secondary industry in Southern Rhodesia was about to create an enormous demand for electric power. Nevertheless, despite a detailed survey, nothing happened until a meeting in 1946 of the Central African Council, established by the British Government in 1944 to extend co-operation and co-ordination between Southern and Northern Rhodesia and Nyasaland. At this meeting, the Council appointed an Inter-Territorial Hydro-Electric Power Commission.

In May 1951, the Commission recommended Kariba as preferable to a similar scheme proposed for the Kafue, for which there were fewer hydrographical records available. Independent consultants from France also said Kariba, the bigger scheme, should come first, with Kafue to follow, and on 1 March 1955, the Federal Prime Minister, Sir Godfrey Huggins, confirmed their choice. There was outrage in the north, where there was great attachment to the Kafue scheme: but there was no going back. The Copperbelt mining companies estimated that by 1960, the mines would face closure if they did not replace their ageing thermal power stations – or have hydro-electric power to draw on. If this challenge was to be met and conquered, there was not a moment to lose.

The building of the Kariba dam was one of the outstanding engineering feats in the history of Africa: a great river, subject to raging floods, to

Kariba: the dam wall. It is higher than St Paul's Cathedral or the Statue of Liberty. It weighs 2,5 million tonnes. Each of its six gates weighs 79 tonnes.

be diverted for the building of a vast dam wall; a narrow gorge with limited working space; temperatures up to 110F and nearly 90 per cent humidity; and first problem of many, a remote, roadless site to supply with hundreds of thousands of tonnes of materials. The World Bank, after close examination, agreed in principle to a loan. The main contract went to an Italian consortium. But there was still no road, time was ticking away, and the preliminary works were vital – a diversion tunnel and channel for the river; the foundations of a coffer dam on the north bank, offices, housing and stores. The race to beat the annual floods began in June 1955: it was narrowly lost. For the 1956 dry season, an all-weather road was essential. Expert opinion said it would take 18 months. Jim Savory, an irrigation engineer, but long familiar with Kariba and with experience of wartime road building, said his men could do it in six months. If he failed, a year's work would be lost. Survey parties worked just ahead of the construction plant, and some stretches made use of tracks made by elephants, who choose their gradients with intelligence. Both water and equipment were short and the work went on day and night. The road was finished in February, at an average rate of seven miles a day, and it never failed.

In April 1956, the World Bank announced the biggest loan in its history – £28,6m. By July, the Federal Government had borrowed the full £80m cost of the first stage of the scheme. In February 1957, the Zambesi gave the first warning of its power – floods that reached the level predicted to happen only once in a thousand years. Even so, in June, the river's flow was turned aside into the diversion tunnel and work began in the vast concrete circles of the coffer dams. But Nyaminyami, the River God, had not finished with the Zambesi. At midnight on 2 March 1958, the river's flow was estimated at 568 000 cubic feet of water a second. It was the ten thousand year flood. Nevertheless, just before midnight on 2 December 1958, the upstream water level was 7m above the downstream level. As the water inched back over the dry earth, millions of crickets crawled out and filled the air with their screeching. Scorpions, mice and shrews climbed on little rafts of grass and twigs. Overhead circled hundreds of birds gathering for the insect feast … By 9 January 1959, Kariba was the biggest man-made lake in Southern Africa. Ten days later it was 150km long, and the game departments of the two Rhodesias began the animal rescue task that became world famous as "Operation Noah."

By June 1959, the vast, curving 2,5m tonne dam wall, 135m high, 653m wide, was completed except for the roadway: six months later, Kariba's first power flowed down the cables to Kitwe from six 115 MW turbines. By the late 1960s, the Copperbelt was beginning to need still more power, and the second stage, the North Bank power station, which doubled Kariba's capacity, was completed in 1976, but not before a long and painful dispute which led to the destruction of the main contracting company.

There were two human tragedies in the building of Kariba. The first and greatest was in the resistance which grew on the north bank of the river among the 34 000 people who would have to be moved to make way for the lake. In September 1958, eight of Chief Chipepo's people were killed and 34 wounded in an armed clash with police. And on 20 February 1959, 17 workmen were killed when a platform collapsed 60m above the ground.

And the name? According to legend, the name should be "Kariwa" – "The Trap." Long ago, there was a great lake behind the hills which eventually broke through, and the fierce torrent tore out the gorge. When the water subsided, it left behind a massive stone slab, the kariwa, which hung between the walls of the gorge until at last it collapsed.

13

THE ZAMBESI

The spelling "Zambeze" is first found on a map in 1680, but as "Zambere" it appeared as early as 1562. The first known reference to any meaning of the name is in a book of 1609 by a Portuguese Dominican friar, Fr. Joao dos Santos, which said that "it takes its rise in a great lake situated in the interior of this Ethiopia … The river is called Zambesi because upon issuing from the lake it turns through a large Kaffir town so called, and from this the river takes the same name as the town …" Livingstone recorded that the Lozi name was "Liambai" and meant "The Big River."

The big river begins as a very small spring bubbling up between the roots of a tree near Kalene Hill in the Mwinilunga District of the North-Western Province, very close to the meeting place of Zambia, Zaire and Angola. It ends 3 540km away in Mozambique – the only major river on the continent of Africa which flows to the east coast. It is the fourth biggest river in Africa after the Nile, the Congo and the Niger, and its basin drains 1 285 million sq km. Within 30km of its origins, the Zambesi becomes a clear, strong river, turning into Angola, then cutting a great arc south-west to re-enter Zambia at Chavuma. Now gathering strength from its tributaries, the Zambesi rushes to the broad sandveld flood plain of the Western Province, then to more rocky country where its course is broken by the Ngonye Falls and numerous rapids, finally emerging into the Caprivi Swamps. Here it is joined by the Chobe river near Kazungula and runs on to the dizzying plunge of the Victoria Falls and the Batoka Gorge, 100km of deep rift, uninhabited, almost unknown, accessible only on foot.

The river emerges to the Gwembe Plain and Lake Kariba; from the spillway at Kariba into another gorge which opens into a wide valley, and here the river is bridged to form a link with Zimbabwe at Chirundu. Soon after, the Kafue pours its water into the Zambesi which now begins a wild, broken tract stretching 100km to the Mpata Gorge, densely forested and rich with game. Below Mpata, the Luangwa joins the Zambesi and the river leaves Zambia for Mozambique. another 160km of mopane forest and the Zambesi reaches Kebrabassa, where the river's once fierce rapids have had their energy turned into electric power.

Not far off is Tete, the river's most ancient township, given a cathedral by the King of Portugal in 1563. From here for half the year the river is navigable for nearly 1 600km to the seven main channels of its delta at. Chinde. In 1497, Vasco da Gama named the Zambesi "The River of Good Signs", and Livingstone, before he was defeated by the barrier at Kebrabassa, called it "God's highway to the interior." It was on the banks of the great river at Shupanga that David Livingstone buried his wife Mary in the shade of a baobab tree on 28 April 1862. In the modern world, it is his river more than anyone else's, for despite all his failures, his ideas brought a dramatic change to the history of Africa.

At the river's source at Kalene Hill, a memorial was unveiled on 24 October 1964. "... This monument stands at the source of the Zambesi River from which Zambia derives its name, and which, with its great tributaries, has played so large a part in the life and history of its people and commemorates the birth of a new nation in which all people are born free, equal and united."

14

KAZUNGULA, THE MEETING POINT

*T*he Eastern Caprivi Zipfel is commonly known as the Caprivi Strip. Zipfel means "tassel" in German, and Count Georg Leo von Caprivi was the German Chancellor in 1890. He succeeded Bismarck, who had reluctantly given way to German nationalist demands to join the "Scramble for Africa" and claimed the inhospitable and then almost unknown south-west of Southern Africa in 1884. An Anglo-German Convention in 1894 gave Germany Heligoland in exchange for Zanzibar, and to Cecil Rhodes's disgust, recognised a German frontier in the south-west which included access to the middle Zambesi by a strip of territory "which shall at no point be less than 20 English miles in width."

The Strip was part of the kingdom of Lewanika of Bulozi, and was demanded by the Germans for no good reason, since the Victoria Falls rendered the river useless for navigation. It was for no better reason that after the Germans were defeated in the First World War, the Strip was not returned to the Lozi, but handed to South Africa in 1920 as part of a League of Nations mandate over South-West Africa.

Between the wars, the Strip was virtually inaccessible from South Africa, and Bechuanaland, which exercised a nominal supervision, considered it "beyond the police area." The only inhabitants were a few Bushmen and a handful of whites, adventurers and men of doubtful reputation – men like "Ben Jonson" as he called himself. He had come to the Strip as a soldier in 1914–15, one of the band of scouts whose task had been to prevent any attempt by German troops in South-West Africa to join Von Lettow's little army in East Africa. He stayed on to become a poet published by leading journals in London, a hunter and trader who made himself virtually king of the Strip and far into Southern Angola. He had a sad end: after shooting a challenger for his powers, he became depressed, distributed his belongings among his followers, and shot himself.

At the outbreak of war in 1939, the South African Government posted a magistrate, Major L.F.W. Trollope, to the Strip to establish law and order from Katima Mulilo opposite Sesheke on the Zambesi. This he did, and became famous for the modern lavatory he installed in a huge baobab behind his office. Trollope loved the Strip, resigned rather than accept a transfer, and spent the rest of his life there. After the Second World War, the United Nations terminated the South African mandate over South-West Africa. But international law sensibly acknowledges the distinction between lawful sovereignty and the actual exercise of authority and accepted the fact of South African rule. The Caprivi Strip, which Trollope himself conceded should "logically form part of Northern Rhodesia", continued to stick an uncompromising finger between Angola and Bechuanaland.

But the finger comes to a sharp point at which the boundaries of what are now Zambia, Namibia, Zimbabwe and Botswana are very close together. Owing to an imperfect knowledge of the geography of the area in 1890, the definition of the boundary of the Strip from the point at which it leaves the Chobe River to run westwards to its intersection with the 21st degree of east longitude was left imprecise and ambiguous. Neither then nor later did any of the parties agree whether or not there is a border between Zambia and Botswana. Before the First World War, it is said that a trader greatly flourished by living on Kankumba Island, where the Zambesi and the Chobe meet, and refusing to recognise the authority – or the taxes – of any of the four governments until one of them could prove ownership.

In 1970, South Africa was attempting to buttress apartheid by creating a buffer zone of subservient states – and one of the most important of these was Botswana. Its government was openly threatened with sanctions. Zambia, herself threatened by Ian Smith's illegal regime in Rhodesia, found in Botswana a willing ally. The ferry across the river at Kazungula developed a new significance. The United States promised a road to link Botswana with Zambia, and, most importantly, a bridge at Kazungula, giving real power to Botswana's only link with independent Africa. South Africa, which had never taken much interest in the ferry, now stated firmly there was no border between Zambia and Botswana. Pretoria could see that Botswana's cattle, then her only export, could be trucked and not trekked to the north, and that the prospect of a railway connection to Dar es Salaam offered an outlet for the products of Botswana's promised mining industry. Her independence of South Africa would become much more of a reality.

In the Times of Zambia in May 1970, Prof. J.I. Craig, of the University of Zambia, argued persuasively and in detail that there is such a border, and thus the site for a bridge. But though the road was built, the bridge never has been, and even with the best of ferries, Kazungula remains an under-used highway for trade and travel. But on 19 July 1995, the Times of Zambia published a feature article on Namibia which spoke of plans for a highway running from Livingstone to Sesheke, across a bridge over the river to Katima Mulilo, through the Caprivi Strip, and on to Walvis Bay via Windhoek – 2 000km from Lusaka. At last, a hundred years on, Count Caprivi's Zipfel may have found its role in the history of Zambia, Namibia, Botswana and Zimbabwe.

15

WAR ON LAKE TANGANYIKA

anganyika, at 660km, is the longest freshwater lake in the world. At its southern tip are Zambia's only port, Mpulungu, and the resorts of the Sumbhu National Park. Eighty years ago, when the First World War broke out in August 1914, Lake Tanganyika formed the border between what were then the Belgian Congo and German East Africa. The Germans, under their formidable commander Von Lettow Vorbeck, far better prepared for war than the British or the Belgians, had two armed vessels on the Lake and a third, larger and more formidable, nearing completion. The only rail connection with the Lake was in German territory at Kigoma. At the outbreak of war, the Germans quickly seized the initiative on the Lake and sank a Belgian steamer near Kigoma in late August before there were even thoughts of arming it. Sailing south, they destroyed the remains of the old missionary steamer The Good News, and the hull of another, the Cecil Rhodes. With unchallenged supremacy on the Lake, the Germans could now easily cut off any Allied force advancing into German territory by landing a seaborne force behind them. John Lee, a hunter and prospector who knew the country intimately, went to London to persuade the Admiralty of the importance of gaining ascendancy on the Lake if the East African campaign was to be won.

As a result, an extraordinary campaign was mounted. It was led by an eccentric, middle-aged naval officer, Commander Spicer-Simson, who was allocated a small naval and military party to transport secretly and to operate on the Lake, two fast, manoeuvrable 12m launches driven by twin 100hp petrol engines. They were armed with 3pdr guns forward and machine guns aft, acetylene searchlights, small mines and small arms. Spicer-Simson jocularly christened them Mimi and Toutou, French colloquial names for cat and dog. They were to be transported complete to their launching on the Lake since assembly on the Lake shore would undoubtedly have been seen by or reported to the Germans.

The party sailed on 15 June 1915 for Cape Town, and after a few days' preparation, loaded the launches and their trailers on a special train which set off for the railhead at Fungurume in the Belgian Congo. John Lee had already surveyed a route to the Lualaba River, and a rough track was being cleared for two steam traction engines from Elisabethville to pull the launches to the Lualaba, 250km through the bush. Bridges – about 150 of them – were made by filling the crossings with logs and poles; the gradients were often steep and both engines, cable traction, teams of oxen and hundreds of labourers were often needed to haul the loaded trailers up the hills and to let them down. It was 28 September when the first traction engine dragged Mimi into Sankisia, where a narrow-gauge railway ran 30km to Bukama and the Lualaba river steamer.

After a week on the river, the expedition arrived at Kabalo, the railhead for their destination, Albertville on Lake Tanganyika. There was no harbour, and they had to build the last 5km of railway line before the vessels were finally launched on 22 and 23 December, 1915, six months after their departure from Britain. They had not long to wait for action. The Germans knew nothing of Spicer-Simson's presence, but suspected the Belgians of building a warship. On Boxing Day, the German vessel Kingani came on a reconnaissance of the lake shore, and the Mimi and Toutou set out on a surprise attack. A shell hit the Kingani's foredeck, killing the captain and two petty officers: another struck the bunker. Listing badly she surrendered.

She was made seaworthy, fitted with a Belgian 12pdr forward and a 3pdr aft and renamed Fifi. When the Hedwig von Wissman appeared on 9 February 1916, Spicer-Simson's little flotilla set out and sank her with one of the last of the Fifi's 12pdr shells. The third German vessel, and by far the biggest, was the Von Gotzen, of 800 tonnes displacement, twenty times the size of the Mimi and Toutou. Now completed and fully armed, she came down the Lake to find out what had happend to the Hedwig and to seek revenge. To the fury of his men, Spicer-Simson refused to leave port. In the end, she was attacked from the air by seaplanes, and when, on 28 July 1916, the Belgians captured Kigoma, they found the Germans had carefully greased the Von Gotzen's machinery and scuttled her in shallow water. She was raised after the war for the Tanganyika Railways, and as the Liemba, still sails between Mpulungu and Kigoma.

16

LAKE MWERU

$\mathcal{L}$ake Mweru, in the remote, extreme north-west of Zambia, is a shallow sheet of water about 130km long and about 45km at its greatest width. It is fed by two large rivers, the Luapula and the Kalungwishi, and drained by the Luvua at the north end. Through the middle of the Lake runs an invisible line – the international boundary between Zambia and Zaire, settled by the Anglo-Belgian Boundary Commission in 1911–14. On the south-western shore, the boundary makes a U-turn to include within Zambia the biggest of the three islands in the Lake, Kilwa, with its cliffs and bat-haunted caves. Kilwa is Zambian because two officials of the BSA Company planted the Union Jack there in the 1890s, forestalling by a couple of days a Belgian party hurrying on the same mission. Perhaps that is why the Zambian share of Mweru is 58 per cent of the total surface area of 4 580 sq km.

The first outsiders to see Mweru were almost certainly the Arab slavers, for the region was notorious as an assembly point for slaves to begin the long march to the coast. The first European to see it was Livingstone, who arrived on 8 November 1867. It has one curious distinction. The first boma to be opened in what became Zambia was built on the Chiengi Stream, and it was probably opened in 1890 rather than 1891, and named by its founder, Richard Crawshay, as "Rhodesia." It was thus one of the first uses of the name anywhere. Not long after its founding, Chiengi suffered its first abandonment, and about 1894, a new station was opened at the mouth of the Kalungwishi River. For a while it took over the name Rhodesia from Chiengi.

Chiengi was described by an early occupant as "a place of singular natural beauty," looking over the Lake to the mountains where the Luapula leaves it to become the Lualaba and at last the Congo river. But Chiengi Boma had a chequered history and a reputation for being haunted: it was usually a one-man station, breeding eccentricity through loneliness, and there was more than one sad tale to tell of it. After several closings and reopenings, it was finally abandoned in 1933. The few visitors who came thereafter found it an eerie place of unhappy atmosphere.

But Chiengi was not all gloom, and in its earlier years, before the invasion of modern commerce, it was the centre of a flourishing industry for the extraction of salt by evaporation from the mud of the Lake's tributary streams. The main interest, however, of the Luapula and the Lake has always been fishing. Commercial exploitation of the lake began about 1928 with Greek fishermen from Zaire who built boats at Kasenga, wove their own nets, and drove their catches packed in ice to sell in what is now Lubumbashi. Today, after intense involvement with the markets of the Zambian and Zairean Copperbelts for over 80 years, the Mweru-Luapula fishery is one of the most advanced in Zambia – though overfishing has caused the disappearance of some species and serious declines in others. One of the losses was the so-called "Luapula Salmon", Mpumbu, once described as "this famous and beautiful fish." It was most vulnerable on its mass annual spawning run, the Kapata, when gravid fish crammed the river and were killed in thousands, not least to feed a Belgian taste for caviar made from the ripe eggs.

There used to be a legend that the run was led by a monster – half fish, half animal, called Akankunkubu. Both the fish and the legend are now gone.

ANIMALS, INSECTS AND FISH

17

KAPENTA

K apenta, that small silvery fish, is one of the most popular foods
in Zambia. It came first to the line of rail from Lake Tanganyika,
where it was caught and sun-dried. Now it comes frozen as well, and from
Kariba, which was wisely stocked with it soon after the lake was formed.
Science knows kapenta as a member of a world-wide family, *Clupeidae*,
among which are numbered the seafish herrings and sardines, greatly
prized for their tasty, oily flesh. Lake Tanganyika is home to two of the
few freshwater representatives of the family, *C. limnothrissa* and *C.
stolothrissa* which have contrived a unique evolution in a habitat of internal drainage separated from other sources of fish species, and in the great
depths occurring naturally in the Rift Valley lake. In Lake Tanganyika,
they occur in commercial quantities, but there are small numbers of three
other species in Lake Mweru. Like other herrings, kapenta are attracted
by lights at night.

Forty years ago, a visitor to Lake Tanganyika described the industry
as it then was – before the name "kapenta" was used: "Nshembe or indagaa are similar to very small sardines, and are usually caught when there
is no moon and the lake is sufficiently calm. Each boat has a small metal
brazier fixed forward of the bows, in which a slow-burning, charcoal-like
wood is burnt. The fish are attracted by the light, and are scooped up in a
net similar to a huge butterfly net, made of mosquito netting. An expert
fisherman and his mates may sometimes catch several tons of fish in the
course of a single 'darkness', and when a large number of boats is out, the
lake is a mass of twinkling lights, and the whole effect most beautiful ..."

A scientist, Dr. S.H. Skaife, wrote in 1951 that the "indagaa" come to
the surface to feed in shoals on the small plants and living creatures floating there, and are then attracted by the fisherman's lights. At dawn, the
fishermen return and the fish "are spread out on the sandy beaches to dry
in the sun – heads, fins, guts and all ..." By 1961, a visiting writer could
say that "all Central Africa knows this tasty fish in its sun-dried form."
With modern fishing craft, electric lights and refrigeration, kapenta has

become even more popular. Nowhere is it more popular than on the Copperbelt, and it is said that it was in the mine townships that it got its name. Because it is so easy to prepare, an idle housewife or girl friend could leave the beerhall with a few minutes to spare before her man came off shift and still have ready for him a tasty plate of fish. And so it became known as "kapenta," the food of the painted women.

18

LECHWE

*L*usaka international airport is Zambia's crossroads and countless thousands over the past quarter century have stopped to admire the statue of the red lechwe fawn with her calf. The statue was commissioned by the Wildlife Conservation Society, wrought by the South African sculptor Coert Steynberg, and unveiled by President Kaunda on 23 October 1967. On the plinth is a quotation from Henry Beston's book "The Outermost House" which says of the creatures of the wild: "They are not brothers, they are not underlings, they are other nations, caught with ourselves in the net of life and time, fellow prisoners of the splendour and travail of the earth."

The choice of lechwe to symbolise the whole wealth of Zambia's wildlife was an appropriate one, for the black lechwe (*Kobus leche smithemani*) is found only around Lake Bangweulu, and the red (*K.l. leche*), though found in small areas of Zaire, Angola and Botswana, is chiefly associated with western Zambia and the Kafue National Park, while the Kafue Flats lechwe (*K.l. kafuensis*) is found only there. A fourth subspecies, *K.l robertsi*, once found along the Luongo River in the Luapula Province, is now extinct. The colloquial name lechwe comes from the Tswana name, leche. It is a medium-sized, reddish-yellow antelope standing about 100cm at the shoulder. The male, who carries lyrate horns which sweep back, out and up to forward-pointing tips, weighs about 100kg, the female about 80kg. With the sitatunga, they are Africa's most water-loving antelope, seldom found more than two or three kilometres from permanent water, in which they are strong swimmers. They are gregarious, forming loose herds from 15–20 animals to huge aggregations of thousands.

Until 1957, the Ila people of the Southern Province used to hunt the lechwe all year round. The biggest drives, called "chila" were held when the flood plains of the Kafue River began to fill each year. Then the dwellers of many villages would combine into a crowd of hundreds to surround the herds of lechwe retreating before the deepening water to slaughter them with spears. Later, as the water deepened and the streams filled, the light hunting dugouts, drawing perhaps three inches of water, came into use. Propelled by ten-foot poles, they flew over the flooded plain, and rarely returned as lightly laden as they went. When the waters retreated, the hunters with their spears and dogs would return; and when the flats were dry and burnt, the young warriors came out to drive the herds and the old men dug concealed pitfalls. And at all times, the lechwe does were specially sought because their skins were prized for making women's petticoats.

Captain Pitman, who carried out the first faunal survey of Northern Rhodesia, recorded in 1932 the "alarming" rate at which the black lechwe was disappearing from the Bangweulu region, due largely, he believed, to the demand for dried meat on the developing mines of the Copperbelt. Protection of lechwe began in 1945, but the herds did not increase. In 1954, a light aircraft was used in a game survey for the first time in Africa; analysis of the photographs it took estimated there were fewer than 20 000 on the flood plains of Lake Bangweulu. Half a century before, hunters spoke of a million. In 1952, it was estimated that 5 000 animals were killed in a single three-day "chila" on the Kafue Flats, and in 1957, recognising the species was facing extinction, the chila was banned.

19
TIGER FISH

*T*he scientific name of the tiger fish is *Hydrocynus vittatus* or "striped water-dog," a description adequate for zoology, but quite inappropriate to this magnificent fish with its streamlined body, silvery sides with jet-black lateral stripes, orange-red fins and large, razor-sharp teeth. It is the most spectacular of Zambia's large freshwater fish, and as a sporting fish it is famous among anglers around the world. It is of great commercial angling and tourist importance; by its voracity it has a profound effect on other fish. A distinguished judge, Sir Robert Tredgold, said that "any fisherman who has not caught a tiger has still something for which to live."

The tiger fish. "Raveningly malignant..." "Any fisherman who has not caught a tiger has still something for which to live..."

Together with the Kafue pike, the tiger fish belongs to a large family of freshwater fish called *Characidae*, related, remarkably enough, to the dreaded piranha of South America – which supports the theory that in very ancient times, South America was close enough to Africa to have a freshwater link between them. But unlike the piranha, though it is attracted by blood in the water, there is no record of it attacking humans or large animals.

There are five species of tiger fish known in Africa, four of them found in the Congo basin, including the "goliath" variety which attains a weight up to some 40kg. In Zambia, despite fishermen's tales, it rarely exceeds 12kg. It has a number of local names – Ngwezhi in the upper Zambesi, Mupenzi in the lower; Nsanga in Bangweulu, Manda at Mweru and Mcheni between the lakes. It is never found in the Kafue.

The angling writer Bernard Venables said of the tiger fish that "no creature is more unremittingly, raveningly malignant than a tiger fish, and that is the means of catching it. You offer it, or pretend to offer it, living flesh …" P.B.N. Jackson, a research scientist, said the laziest and least interesting way of catching them is trolling from a moving boat. "Spinning, from the shore, is very rewarding, and respectable specimens can be caught on a fly." But, he says, "ledgering with a fillet of fish on the bottom … is probably the best way of obtaining a really large tiger …" In the kitchen, the tiger fish has little reputation. According to W.G. Fairweather, who spent his leisure for 40 years fishing around Livingstone, it is very bony and fit only to be pickled or pan-boiled, then filleted and fried.

20

WHITE ANTS

*T*ermites, miscalled "white ants", are the most mysterious and interesting of all insects. There are about 400 different species in Africa alone, 3 500 world-wide. They are capable of immense damage to buildings, furniture, books, gardens and crops. They are low in the order of creation, much lower than true ants, but they have been around, quite unchanged, for perhaps 100 million years, and the termite mound is thus by far the oldest type of organised community on the face of the earth. These "termitaria" can rise like church spires six metres or more from the ground, containing tonnes of soil and creating expensive problems when they have to be removed. Within this relatively colossal structure, built of soil particles cemented with the termites' excrement, millions of them live in the perpetual, air-conditioned darkness essential to their being. Most are blind. Most, too, are workers – stunted, undeveloped males and females that live but to labour. They are not only outstanding builders, but miners too – digging tunnels in all directions in search of decaying wood and humus. Because everything is digested and the excrement used as cement, the interiors of termitaria are spotlessly clean. Surprisingly, termites cannot themselves digest cellulose, but contain micro-organisms that do it for them. Recent research has found that one of the by-products of this digestive process is methane gas – and by their astronomical numbers, the flatulent termites produce a fifth of the world's methane, a potent contributor to global warming.

About five in a hundred of the inhabitants are soldiers, blind and sexually immature like the workers, and needing to be fed by them. Their task is to defend the colony, mainly against ants, with their huge jaws and a gland that produces a sticky irritant fluid. Before the rains each year, most termite mounds contain large numbers of white-coloured nymphs with four white stumps of wings on their backs. These nymphs are specially fed and treated so that they grow into mature males and females, their wings expand, their bodies harden, and two sets of eyes develop. Then, usually in all the mounds in the area at the same time, the walls of the nest are

A termite mound, rising like a church spire, built by creatures with 100 million years of experience.

broken, soldiers appear at the openings, and the winged termites take to their clumsy flight. They cannot fly far, and their predators are many. Mankind finds them tasty eaten alive or fried, chickens adore them, wild birds take them on the wing – never mind the antbear and the pangolin.

The surviving females land first, running around, shedding their wings, then stopping to give off a scent to attract the males. Each pair soon digs a hole and disappears – and a new colony is founded. The so-called "king" is smaller than his mate: his only function to ensure that the "queen", a palpitating, sausage-like creature (memorably described as resembling "a half deflated Zeppelin in a gale"), maintains the stock of fertile eggs – as many as ten thousand a day. If the queen dies or is killed, the workers set about feeding nymphs to provide another.

Among the hundreds of species of termites, there are several broad categories. The harvester termites, for example, do not build above ground level: they can cause damage to lawns, shrubs, crops, wallpaper, books, carpets and clothes in their interminable search for food. Another type, with snouted soldiers, lives in mounds and causes heavy damage to stockfeed crops. In Zambia, many of the "anthills" are occupied by termites which cultivate fungus gardens for their food, and it is these which build the mud-covered runways up the foundations and walls and into the timber of buildings. But the damage caused by termites is far better known than their contribution to the natural economy. They loosen, mix and aerate the soil, their tunnels soak up the rains. They break down immense amounts of dead wood, making its organic matter available to the next generation of plants and animals, and keeping the forest from becoming impenetrable with debris. With this – and much more – known about the termites, they still remain a mystery. Their air-conditioned cities are difficult to create in laboratory conditions: termites are delicate and hard to keep alive. How do the three types of termite develop? Are the eggs different? How is discipline maintained in the crowded nest? Who organises the multitude of activities?

Because they need soil with at least ten per cent clay with which to build, termites are absent from the sands of the Western Province, plentiful in the mopane woodland and the savanna woodland of maize and cattle country, where they are always ready to spring an unpleasant surprise on mankind's precious possessions. Wrote Joseph Edward Hughes of his early days on Lake Bangweulu: "I once had a large Gladstone bag, a relic of my first coming out; this had a handle on top and contained clothing; nothing looked wrong with it, but one day I started to lift it up by the handle, and up came the top and sides like a dish cover. The bottom part of the bag and all the contents had been devoured ..."

21

CHEMBE, THE FISH EAGLE

"At earliest dawn on the Luapula, before the little birds in the trees start their chirruping, the beautiful broad-winged Chembe soars to the skies from his perch to sound the 'reveille' with his shrill, piercing scream … First one bird rings out, in tones audible many miles away, 'Nkoya, Nkoya, Nkoya Kupwa' which means 'I go, I go, I go to get married.' The answering call from his mate is 'Kaweeya, Kaweeya, Kaweeya Kupwa'- Go, Go, Go and get married …" So wrote Joseph Edward Hughes, the naturalist and hunter who lived on Lake Bangweulu from 1908 to 1919.

Chembe's scientific name is *Haliaaetus vocifer*, the African fish eagle, and "vocifer" is a Latin tribute to his loud, cheerful, squealing cry, given with his head thrown back. He is Zambia's national bird, familiar from the coat of arms. He and his mate are found in Africa and along its coasts from Senegal and Ethiopia to the Cape – where the fish eagle was first recorded in 1800. In Zambia as elsewhere, the fish eagle is found wherever there is a large area of water, in lakes, rivers, even quite small dams, though perhaps most commonly associated with the Kafue.

Their colouring is distinctive – white head, back, chest and tail; black wings and scapulars; dark chestnut abdomen, upper and under wing-coverts; yellow eyes, black beak, yellow feet and toes. The breadth of a wing ranges from 47 to 60cm. They build large nests made of sticks, untidily lined with grass or waterweed, and used year after year. The breeding season is May to August and there are usually two white eggs.

Selous, the great hunter, remembered them along the Zambesi – "the handsome white-headed fish-eagle, as he soars in graceful circles high overhead, or, seated on the topmost branch of some withered tree, gives vent from time to time to the loud shrieking cry peculiar to the eagle tribe …" They are often seen making a magnificent swoop at a fish with a tremendous rushing noise, usually checked just before impact with the water, but sometimes going right under to grab the fish with their claws before swooping up with it to a tree branch. Then, as often as not, the eagle drops it, and many a Zambian has taken advantage of this curious habit to snatch a free meal. Hughes says that like otters, fish eagles scale their fish before eating them. They do not always catch their own prey, but will often steal from other fish-catching birds. Occasionally they will eat carrion or the young of other waterside birds. And for sport, they will chase herons, especially, it is said, the huge Goliath heron. Chembe's splendid looks and brave style make him a worthy symbol of the nation.

22

A Fine Fish

There are in the world about 12 000 species of birds and mammals, and about 20 000 varieties of fish. But because of the way they live, fish are difficult animals to study. Long after Zambia's birds, mammals, reptiles and insects had attracted widespread scientific attention, her fish, invisible most of the time, were neglected. It was not until 1934 that the first check list of Zambia's fish was made by Captain C.R.S. Pitman in his pioneering survey of the country's fauna. In 1936, two young science graduates, Kate Ricardo and Janet Owen, came to Northern Rhodesia to spend nine months following up the work of the eminent zoologist, Dr. Barton Worthington, on the fish of several of the great lakes of Central Africa. The Colonial Office, which backed the research, recognised that fish would be of importance in feeding a population already beginning rapid growth. With war intervening, not much more was done until the establishment of the Joint Northern Rhodesia and Nyasaland Fisheries Research Organisation in 1951. Ten years later, its first Chief Fisheries Research Officer, P.B.N. Jackson, stationed at Samfya on Lake Bangweulu, produced the first lengthy, detailed successor to Pitman's pioneering work.

Jackson's researches reinforced the claim that Zambia's fish are among its most valuable natural resources – providing essential animal protein in the diet of millions, employing thousands of fishermen in one of the country's most important rural industries, and forming one of the country's greatest tourist attractions. Though Jackson gave pride of place to the tiger fish as Zambia's most important fish – to angling and tourism as well as through its influence on other fish – he was in no doubt that the genus Tilapia belongs to our most important single family of fishes, the *Cichlidae*, commonly called bream. This is a name which rightly belongs in Europe and to a member of the carp family, "but," said Jackson, "its use for a group of perch-like fishes is so deeply entrenched that nothing short of nuclear warfare, if that, will ever change it."

The Zambian species and sub-species of bream are deep-bodied, broad-headed, medium-sized fish which can grow to 3 kg or more in weight. They are considered intelligent and adaptable, famous for their reproductive capacity – they spawn up to six times a year and a single female may rear up to 5 000 fry in a year. But they are also distinguished by the care they take of their eggs and their young. Most Tilapia are "maternal brooders": the female takes the eggs into her mouth and incubates them there after they have been spawned into and fertilised in a nest made by the male. The eggs hatch after about ten days, but remain in the female's mouth for a further few days. Once the storage yolk is used up, the juveniles make short feeding sorties, seldom straying far, and darting back into her mouth if danger threatens. After another ten days, the female releases the young in warm shallow waters – "nursery areas" – where they feed independently. The flesh of Tilapia is comparatively boneless and of excellent flavour.

All these qualities taken together adapt them outstandingly for fish-farming. They are also popular among anglers, who may take them on light tackle, when they put up as good a fight as most freshwater fish, and they will take a fly at high water when fish are feeding off the grass banks of rivers. They like worms and grasshoppers. In Lake Kariba, they are a popular prey for spear-fishing.

Among the many species of Tilapia found in Zambia, the best-known include *T. mossambica* found in the middle and lower Zambesi and such tributaries as the Luangwa, but not the Kafue. It is found far down in South Africa, even in the salty estuaries of rivers flowing into the sea. Stranger still, it achieved fame as a pond culture fish and was introduced to Indonesia by the Dutch before the Second World War, and distributed by the Japanese occupation forces to Malaysia and Taiwan. Since then it has spread further round the world, and it is doubtless still on its travels. Kariba bream, *Oreochromis mortimeri*, was introduced to Lake Kariba in 1959–61 from the Department of Game and Fisheries' ponds at Chilanga. When the Lake was filling, they became extremely abundant and anglers often caught sackfuls. Since then it has settled down to become the dominant commercial fish.

T. melanoplura, the red-breasted bream, is probably the best-known in Zambia because its wide distribution has been supplemented by man, who has used it to stock waters far from its original habitat. It is not a mouth-breeder, but still guards its young very carefully. In fish culture, it is usually farmed with another species, *macrochir*, the green-headed bream, because between them they make the most of the available plant resources and respond to artificial feeding with all sorts of green stuff and the decaying products of this stimulate the growth of algae which both of them eat.

And the name? The word Tilapia was coined by Sir Andrew Smith ("Report of the Expedition for Exploring Central Africa", 1836) from the word "Tlhapi" (with a click) which means, in the region of the Okavango Swamps, a fish. Since Jackson has nearly 40 entries under Tilapia in his index, it seems a very appropriate name for a national asset.

23

THE YEARS OF THE LOCUST

*I*n November 1930, William Allan, the Northern Rhodesia Government entomologist, posted to the Imperial Institute of Entomology in London some locust wings he had collected in the remote marshes of Lake Mweru, where local people said swarms of locusts had been seen each year since 1927. In 1930, they told him, the swarms had become much bigger. London identified the wings as those of the red locust, *Nomadacris septemfasciata*, hardly known or seen since an outbreak in Uganda in 1915–19. The outbreak at Mweru Wantipa was far worse. It was the beginning of a great locust plague that did not end until 1945, when it had covered three million square miles of southern Africa.

After a disastrous plague affecting the United States and Canada, American research in the 1870s made a vital discovery: all kinds of locusts have permanent breeding areas from which swarms spread out during a plague. When these outbreak areas are identified, they can be watched, breeding discouraged, and methods of killing them established. These permanent breeding areas are only one of the mysteries of migratory locusts. Another is their ability to live in swarms or as individuals, and the strange difference between them. The swarms may be compared to an army: they move, camp, feed and live together – and wear a regulation uniform. Those living singly wear no uniform and appear so unlike locusts that it is difficult to believe they belong to the same species. What to the lay observer appears to be a large grasshopper is a locust on leave.

In favourable conditions in an outbreak area, the solitary locusts multiply rapidly. The female lays eggs in batches of about 100 with the first rains, and generally two or three batches are laid at about fortnightly intervals. After a month, hoppers hatch out and feed on the surrounding vegetation. If they are densely crowded, they begin to form migratory bands – and this is the time to destroy them. Left alone, they turn into winged adults, the migratory instinct develops, and they begin to excite each other into migration.

At Mweru Wantipa in 1930, it was too late to stop this relentless sequence of events. The swarms had already broken out of their permanent breeding area and acquired the ability to multiply on almost any grassland plain, setting in train generation after generation of migrating swarms whose end could not be foreseen. The district commissioner at Chiengi in 1929 called the people out to deal with a large swarm emerging from the marsh, and they ate almost the whole of it. But the swarms were spreading: in 1932, 20 000 men were engaged in killing hoppers around the country, but beating, trenching, burning and sprinkling of arsenic powder made little impression on the plague. In 1933 there was a tremendous spreading of swarms throughout both Rhodesias, Nyasaland, Mozambique and South Africa. It was a disastrous blow to countries already suffering bitterly from the world depression.

A swarm weighing 1 000 tonnes was not uncommon, and the biggest were estimated at 50 000 tonnes. Locusts consume about ten times their own weight while growing, and a migrating swarm of 1 000 tonnes will eat its own weight in vegetation in a day. In areas of cultivation, locust damage was often dramatic, sudden, bankrupting. In a typical case, the entire maize crop on several Chisamba farms was consumed: Northern Rhodesia lost a fifth of its 1933 crop. Among peasant farmers, famine was a grim reality. In some remote places, the old people were sent out into the bush to fend for themselves on roots and bulbs; few survived for long. No-one who has seen the huge mass of a swarm darkening the sky for miles will ever forget it. As they land, every blade of grass bends under the weight of the insects, trees and branches become shimmering pillars of them, and the air is filled with the rustling of their wings. And when they leave, the land is desolated. Motorists driving into a swarm found their windscreens blinded with crushed locusts, their radiator grilles filled and the engines overheating. The driving wheels of locomotives spun in the greasy mass of crushed insects on the line.

The greatest extent of the plague was reached in 1935, when it covered three million square miles. By this time, entomologists were converging on two similar outbreak areas – Mweru Wantipa and the Rukwa Valley of Tanganyika, both valleys with closed drainage. Both were hot, remote, inhospitable. When the governments of the outbreak area decided on co-operation in 1949, the International Red Locust Control Service was established at Abercorn in the cool highlands. With better insecticides and mechanical spraying – including aircraft – breeding swarms were almost completely controlled: the few that escaped were pursued and destroyed. After 1935, the plague slowly waned, though it continued for another ten years, and outbreaks were only narrowly averted in 1947 and 1951. Chemical control in the permanent breeding areas was supplemented by ecological research – to find out what conditions create the permanent breeding areas, and to change them – and this continues. Research since 1949, and since 1970 by the renamed International Red Locust Control Organisation for Central and Southern Africa, has shown there is a total of six outbreak areas for the red locust. In addition to Mweru Wantipa and the Rukwa Valley, the list now includes the Kafue Flats, the Wembere Steppe and the Malagarasi river basin in Tanzania, and the plains of Lake Chilwa in Malawi. Until all the answers to the mysteries of the locust are found, the price of freedom from them is, like freedom itself, eternal vigilance.

24

A DOSE OF FEVER

*U*ntil a century ago, malaria protected the interior of Africa from invasion and outside influence, retarding the development of both indigenous and expatriate populations more than any other single factor. The disease has been known and feared from the dawn of history, and its very name, meaning "bad air", arose from the belief that the infection came from the poisonous miasmas of the southern Italian marshes. Europe first heard of a treatment for the fever in 1638, when the wife of the Spanish Viceroy of Peru, Count Cinchon, was clearly dying of an intermittent fever. In desperation, the court physician suggested the use of a remedy from the Indians of the northern Andes, an infusion of quinquina bark. The Countess was cured, and in her honour the genus of the tree was named Cinchona. On her return to Europe in the 1640s, she employed quinquina bark to control the endemic fevers of her husband's estate.

David Livingstone, a doctor of medicine, was convinced by his travels that by careful choice of area, and adequate dosage of quinine, it was possible for Europeans to live and flourish in the Far Interior and to bring "Christianity and Commerce" to it. The development of plantations of cinchona trees in the 19th century made quinine abundant, but it was only part of the answer, and an unacceptably high proportion of the brave men and women who answered Livingstone's call knew beyond doubt that the likeliest outcome of their endeavours would be martyrdom to disease. Holloway Helmore led a party of missionaries to Linyanti, arriving in February 1859, the worst month of the year for fever. Within two months, Helmore and his wife were dead, the wife of Roger Price, the other missionary, and five out of seven children. Only Price and two Helmore children survived to make a long and dreadful journey back to the south. So swift and numerous were the deaths that Price was convinced the Makololo had poisoned them. Ironically, the Makalolo themselves, who had come from the fever-free Basutoland in 1823, suffered bitterly from malaria, and their chief, Sekeletu, complained to Livingstone in 1853 that his people were dying out.

It was not until 1897-8 that Sir Ronald Ross proved the transmission of malarial parasites by mosquito bite, and even longer before its general acceptance. The famous hunter Denis Lyell, writing as late as 1910, believed only that the connection with mosquito bites had been proved "almost conclusively," and he still believed that "a stiff dose of calomel, followed by Epsom salts, will drive away an impending attack, and care should be taken to keep the bowels in working order." This was not far removed from Livingstone's famous "Rouser" of half a century before, which added jalap, calomel and rhubarb to quinine, with Epsom salts to follow if necessary. But by the early years of this century, washing down quinine with whisky at sundown was a common practice among settlers, and they bore with fortitude the unpleasant bouts of malaria, with its frightful aches and pains and its chills and fevers, that broke through this defence.

The most dangerous of the malarial parasites is *Plasmodium falciparum*, the source of malignant tertian malaria, a form frequently fatal when it attacks the brain or liver. Alive, but unfortunate, were the victims of chronic malaria, anaemic, feeble and thin, with enlarged liver and spleen, subject to doses of fever year in and out. They were usually people who lived an irregular life, who took quinine only when they felt a dose of fever coming on. For them in particular there was a greater danger, blackwater fever, which also developed from the *falciparum* infection, and was characterised by haemoglobinuria, "black water." The death rate ranged from one to five out of every ten cases. Probably because of this terrible reputation, a great mass of superstition grew up around blackwater. One of the most persistent was the belief that the victim must on no account be moved, but must have shelter built over him in which to consume huge amounts of grain beer. In more elevated social circles, it was held that champagne was the sovereign specific for blackwater, and it was not until the 1930s, during the governorship of Sir James Maxwell, who had entered the administration by way of the colonial medical service, that the official issue of a few half bottles to boma medicine cupboards was summarily ended. But surprisingly often it proved true that moving a blackwater patient would kill him.

How did the mythology of blackwater arise? No Zambian ever suffered from it, and the European experience of Africa was only a few decades long. The most likely explanation is that knowledge of blackwater came to Africa from the first attempt to cut the Panama Canal, when yellow fever and malaria defeated the contractors in 1881–9. There is little doubt that it is a development of malignant tertian malaria, and actively promoted by irregular dosage of quinine. With the development of better drugs, blackwater virtually disappeared, and with the discovery of residual insecticides for long-term mosquito control, malaria itself could be controlled without difficulty in urban areas.

Nowhere was this more forcibly demonstrated than on the Copperbelt. When development of the first mine began at Luanshya in 1927, the mosquitoes breeding in the swamps around the Luanshya stream took a fearful toll of the newly-recruited labour force, and the entire project was threatened. In 1929, Chester Beatty, one of the founding fathers of the Copperbelt, took a bold decision and called in the Ross Institute of Tropical Hygiene in London. Bold because it was still widely held by scientists that mosquito eradication was far too expensive and prone to failure in comparison with eliminating the parasites by dosing their human carriers with quinine. Sir Malcolm Watson, director of the Ross Institute, devised a brilliant, inexpensive and wholly successful campaing of controlling mosquito breeding, and solved a problem approaching that of the Panama Canal, of which it was said that "if we had failed to control malaria we would have failed to build the Canal".

25

NSULU, THE HONEY-GUIDE

"The habits of this species have probably provoked more discussion than those of any other African bird," it was said by those distinguished ornithologists Mackworth-Praed and Grant. Indeed, the quaintness of its scientific name provokes an instant need to know more: *Indicator indicator*. It is in fact a very appropriate name for "a rather drab, insignificant bird about the size of a common sparrow" as Norman Carr calls it, for it leads man – or honey badgers – to bees' nests. "Now is the time for honey" – the new season's honey – wrote Joseph Edward Hughes of the month of December, "the honey guide birds coming daily in threes and fours to bring the news …" Nsulu twitters anxiously around, flitting away a little distance to a perch, and then returns chattering like rattling a half-empty matchbox or squeaking like rubbing a wet finger on a window-pane to entice a helper, for the hive is often found deep in the centre of a tall hollow tree with only a small aperture which must be chopped open to get at the honey. It is easy to follow Nsulu, for as he darts from tree to tree, awaiting his helper, he shows his white tail feathers like a rear light, calls more loudly if there is any deviation from the proper course, and hovers excitedly when the hive is reached. He has no fear of the bees, and this may be due to his curiously tough skin, perhaps impervious to stings.

Then a fire is made at the base of the tree, green fuel is added to make it smoke profusely and stupefy the bees. If there are no convenient branches, a few forked poles will make a rough ladder. With a few deft strokes of the axe the hive is opened by the honey gatherer who reaches in to grab chunks of honeycomb to throw down to his companions. What is not eaten on the spot is carried in bark containers, but not before Nsulu is rewarded. All over Africa, Nsulu is always left wax grubs and honey for his own consumption. It is said that if the offering is not left, Nsulu will lead the miscreant to unwanted meetings with unfriendly animals. On the other hand, for hunters, Nsulu can be an infuriating nuisance, for his loud pleadings are heard by the prey, which sensibly associates them with humans – and guns.

Nsulu depends on man for help with his food, and on other birds to bring up his offspring: like the cuckoo, he and his mate are parasites, laying their shiny white eggs in the nest holes of other species, and, it is believed, often pecking small holes in their host's eggs.

TREES, FLOWERS AND PARKS

26

KAFUE NATIONAL PARK

Concern for the preservation of threatened species in Africa has a surprisingly long history. The Transvaal Republic approved a game preservation bill in 1846, and the Sabie Reserve there was established in 1898. By 1900, the destruction of the once almost limitless herds of American bison and the consequent establishment of the first national park – Yellowstone – had resounded round the world. They led to a conference in London which recognised the dramatic effect of the extending "gun frontier" on Africa's game: that many of the vast herds seen by Livingstone were already on course for extinction within a few generations. The conference listed animals deserving of protection and proposed the establishment of game reserves. In Northern Rhodesia, the first to be declared was Kafue, in 1924.

In 1931, Capt. Charles Pitman, a much-decorated ex-Indian Army officer who had become Game Warden for Uganda, was seconded to Northern Rhodesia for two years to carry out a faunal survey and to recommend a site for the country's first national park. He considered the Luangwa Valley, Mweru Marsh and the area around the Livingstone Memorial, but rejected them in favour of Kafue, a decision pressed on him by the then district commissioner at Mumbwa, Rowland Hudson, who was to rise to high office in the Ministry of Overseas Development in London.

Zambia has set aside more land than any other in Africa for the preservation of its natural resources. In 1950, Kafue was the first of its 19 National Parks. It is also by far the largest, covering 22 400sq km which makes it fourth largest in the world after Buffalo in Canada, Gemsbok in Botswana and Salonga in Zaire. Pitman's choice of Kafue for the first of them was influenced not only by its rich variety of wild life, but equally because it had very few human inhabitants, and these were comfortably resettled just east of the Nalusanga entry gate. In this way, Government was able to set aside an area bigger than Wales for the preservation of wild life without disturbing human activity.

The Kafue National Park stretches across land in the Central, North-Western and Southern Provinces. It stretches over a vast plateau watered by two tributaries of the Kafue, the Lunga and the Lufupa. In the north, towards Kasempa, the park is on the flat, open Busanga Plain, surrounded by swamps draining into the Lufupa – scenery found only in that part of Zambia, and with the Park's greatest array of wildlife. For 200km, the Park keeps pace with the great Kafue River itself until it makes its turn towards the Zambesi and the sea.

Kafue is best known for the richness of its bird life, and along the Kafue and the Lufupa for the excellence of its fishing. The game is never concentrated as it is along the Luangwa towards the end of the dry season, and visitors must travel more to see game; and unlike the Luangwa, the Kafue Park is entirely on the plateau country, between 970 and 1 470m above sea level, and between sandy south and swampy north it is generally flat to gently undulating, with a few small hills mainly in the central section. Miombo woodland with its open grassland damboes dominates much of the Park. In the southern sector there are areas of mopane woodland and a few patches of teak forest. In the extreme north is the Busanga Plain, merging into swamps, and here is the greatest variety of wild animals and of waterfowl. The most abundant animals in the Park are buffalo and hartebeest. Reedbuck, waterbuck, puku and impala are common near the major rivers, and elephant, zebra, warthog, roan and sable, eland, oribi, duiker, baboons and vervet monkeys are widely distributed. Lion, leopard, cheetah, hyaena, jackal and wild dog are there too, with lion and leopard particularly common.

In the south, near Namwala, man has made his most serious mark on the almost untouched scenery of the Park – the building of the Itezhi-Tezhi Dam which feeds the Kafue hydro-electric scheme. The dam is outside the Park, but the lake at high water covers 370sq km, mainly up the Musa River, within the Park. Nearby is the Park's biggest camp, Ngoma Lodge, and its airstrip.

Jukes Curtis, a trader and transporter who lived at Mumbwa for many years, dreamed of putting on the river a replica of the huge, shallow-draft sternwheel paddle steamers that plied on the Mississipi. From the decks of such a floating hotel, visitors would be able to watch game along a 100km stretch of river. One day, perhaps …

27

THE BAOBAB

The first reference to the baobab that the Oxford Dictionary can find was in 1592 when it was reported from "Aethiopia." But it was after Michel Adanson, a French botanist who saw it in Senegal in 1754 that it was given its scientific name, *Adansonia digitata*. "I perceived a tree of prodigious thickness," he wrote. "I do not believe the like was ever seen in any part of the world." Its strange appearance – Livingstone thought it looks like a giant carrot planted upside down – has given it legendary status, and one tale was solemnly recorded by the hunter and naturalist, Joseph Edward Hughes …"As far back as 1902 … Namungomba, pointing with his spear to an object on the ground, said 'Mlambi Ulya', meaning 'a Baobab.' The object he was pointing at was a horrible-looking shaky creeper fifteen or sixteen feet long, which was growing along the ground and making its way in the direction of a large tree. It was round, without branch or leaf, and was covered with the same smooth purplish-brown bark as the well-known big tree … Namungomba told me that this creeper slowly coils itself round and eventually engulfs a large tree, changing into the hideous, well-known big tree. Both parent and child have a sinister, awesome appearance. I did not know that this was an original discovery until this year, 1932, when in the course of conversation with the authorities at Kew, it came to light that it was unknown to them there that the Baobab starts life as a creeper. They knew that other big trees start life that way, and they also mentioned that it was an old saying that no one had ever seen a young baobab …" In fact young baobabs are often seen, and it is recorded that an optimistic agriculture officer once planted an avenue of them to shade him in his old age.

Whatever the legends, it is truly a long-lived tree. A huge one cut down while Kariba Dam was being built proved to be just over 1 000 years old. It is also one of the most useful. The baobab's wood is soft, spongy and of little use to man except for fishing floats, but the inner bark can be used for making bark cloth, bark rope for game nets, and wadding for tamping down the powder in muzzle-loading guns. The

Like a giant carrot planted upside down, thought Livingstone – the baobab tree.

melon-like seed pods can be used as snuff boxes, as water carriers, or carved into curios. The seeds are in a white pulp which makes a nourishing, if sour porridge, and the seeds, which contain some tartaric and citric acid – it is often called the Cream of Tartar tree – make a lemonade-like drink. The seeds can also be roasted like groundnuts – though it is said that these make the eater more attractive to crocodiles – and the young leaves can be used like spinach or made into soup. The naturalist Norman Carr has recorded that elephant, during cycles of population increase, will feed off the fibrous trunk of the baobab, probably in search of calcium. The huge trunk of the baobab – it can grow to 20m or more in circumference – has led to its occasional use for storage, and a number of medicinal and magical uses have been recorded. One of the strangest transformations was contrived by the one-time administrator of the Caprivi Strip, who turned one into a lavatory complete with water flush. About the only part of the baobab which is of no use to mankind are the large white flowers which smell of rotten meat – probably intended by nature to entice bats and bluebottles for pollination.

28

THE LUANGWA NATIONAL PARKS

A Luangwa Game Reserve was declared on the east bank of the river on 31 December 1904, doubtless at the instigation of the then Administrator of North-Eastern Rhodesia, Robert Codrington, a dedicated amateur scientist and collector. It lapsed after his departure and death in 1908, and was not revived for thirty years, when a Luangwa Valley Game Reserve was declared in May 1938. It then covered roughly the area of the present South Luangwa, National Park No.1, which was named and enlarged in February 1972. It now covers 9 050sq km. of the mid-Luangwa Valley, bounded by an escarpment on the west and the Luangwa River on the east. The Valley is home to elephant and lion, crocodiles, buffalo, hippo, impala, puku, zebra, waterbuck, warthog, baboons and vervet monkey. It is also home to two isolated sub-species named after the early Government officials who first reported them – Cookson's wildebeest and Thornicroft's giraffe. (It is said that in his old age, "Dongolosi" Thornicroft would spend hours in front of the stuffed specimen in the Natural History Museum in London, hoping for a chance to tell how he shot it.)

The Luangwa is part of the Great Rift Valley, and the river runs through it for 660km until it joins the Zambesi. Along the river, some 650m below the plateau, it is far hotter, and the vegetation changes to the mopane woodland beloved of the elephants, and host to the much-prized mopane worm, an edible moth caterpillar. Beneath the Valley, among the ancient rocks, have been found the petrified remains of reptiles and fossilised trees; Stone Age man lived there too, and long after, three centuries ago, Portuguese explorers passed this way, leaving behind, as proof of their passing, a cannon. Modern man, as he so often does, has brought the greatest change to the Valley's isolation ... At the height of the dry season, the pools and streams dry up, and only the river, itself reduced to a relative trickle, provides water for the profusion of wild animals and birds which lives in the valley. This concentration of game has brought the Luangwa Valley world-wide fame, and its value to the local economy was first recognised by Chief Nsefu who opened the first tourist camp in 1949. Others followed between 1955 and 1972, and a new airport, Luangwa bridge and all-weather roads opened in 1975.

The North Luangwa National Park No.2, also declared in 1972, covers 4636 sq km and is woodland without the open grassy plains of the south park. Wild animals are as abundant as in the south, but it is kept as a wilderness area, and except for a simple access track there is no visitor road system and only designated camping areas. The Luambe National Park No.4, at 254 sq km one of the smallest, has its western boundary along the Luangwa, opposite the corridor separating the North and South Parks. Before its declaration as a national park in 1972 , it was a game reserve created in 1954 under an agreement with Chief Luambe, like Chief Nsefu a pioneer of tourist development in the Eastern Province.

The best-known inhabitant of the Luangwa Valley, the naturalist and former game warden Norman Carr, refined its reputation with his "wilderness trails" in which small parties of visitors take a walking tour experiencing close contact with the Valley's flora and fauna. Camping at night in the wilderness, Carr has written, brings "the companionship of a camp fire, the smell of mopane smoke, and the talk of shared adventures against a backdrop of African night noises ... an atmosphere difficult to simulate, but once you have experienced it you are near to finding infinite contentment ..."

29

THE STORY OF MUNDA WANGA

"Munda Wanga" means "My Garden." It was the name given by Ralph Sander to the first five acres he leased from Government near his job at the then Game & Tsetse Control Department at Chilanga. It was 1952, and Sander, a bachelor in his 40s who joined the Forest Department in 1948 before transferring to Chilanga, had a dream of creating not just a garden but a botanical showpiece. The land had a derelict hut on it, but much more important, a stream of water running through it. Sander came of a well-known horticultural family in England and was himself a member of the Royal Horticultural Society. He had ideas and skills – but very little money. (Years later, he claimed he had once had to choose between a wife and the garden because he could not afford both: the garden won.) He moved into the hut and began to make his dream come true.

With the help of three part-time gardeners, Sander laboured before he went to work, after he came back from work, and all through the weekends. It took him six years to clear the bush and lay out the gardens, using no more than spades and wheelbarrows. Then he persuaded Government to lease him a further 12 acres and the building society to lend him enough money to build ornamental bridges, a summerhouse, lawns and terraces, to plant trees and shrubs – and to sink a borehole to provide the water he needed for pools, waterfalls and streams. And, as an employee of the Game Department, Sander took additional pleasure in creating a sanctuary for animal orphans of the wild and an aviary for young and injured wild birds.

By 1962, Ralph Sander's single-minded devotion to Munda Wanga had devoured not only most of his salary; he had cashed in his life insurance, commuted his pension and sold most of his possessions. But it was still not enough to keep the gardens going, and he had a long battle with unsympathetic authority before he was given permission, as a civil servant, to charge the public for admission. By 1964, Munda Wanga covered

40 acres, there was a staff of nine and a collection of over 50 000 trees, shrubs, climbers and plants – probably the most exensive in Africa. Ralph Sander died in 1978 at the age of 69, and the ownership of Munda Wanga passed into the hands of Government. In 1982, it was taken over by the National Hotels Development Corporation with plans to turn it into a "multi-purpose recreation centre." But money was scarce, and there was now no-one with Ralph Sander's passionate commitment: in June 1987, President Kaunda said he was "appalled" at its run-down condition. Not much has changed since then, but in 1995, it was listed for privatisation, and perhaps, somewhere, there is another Ralph Sander awaiting the challenge.

Ralph Sander's garden – Munda Wanga – home for 50 000 trees and plants.

30

THE VEGETABLE
IVORY PALM

In southern Zambia, mostly below a line stretching roughly from Mongu via Mumbwa and Mkushi to Lundazi, you will often see tall palm trees with fan-shaped leaves and one or more swellings in their trunks. The fruits, which mature about September to November, are round, red-brown and glossy. Inside is a brown, spongy layer which is edible and tastes like gingerbread. Then, inside a very hard fibrous covering, there is a white, onion-shaped seed about 2,5cm in diameter which contains a little milk when fresh. But soon it becomes extremely hard and for this reason it is called "vegetable ivory." It has been used for making buttons, brooches and ornaments and the heads of walking sticks.

The scientific name for the vegetable ivory palm is *Hyphaene ventricosa*, but it has many Zambian names. The Forest Department's book "Know Your Trees" lists 19, including lubali (Bemba), mulala (Lozi, Tonga, Nyanja) and kambili (Kaonde). Apart from vegetable ivory, these palms have other useful properties. It has a handsome wood which can be polished, is proof against borers and is often used for making the rafters of a house. The fruits, seedlings and shoots can be eaten, the sap can be drunk as palm wine or distilled to produce spirit. The leaves make mats and baskets, and the fibres can be made into string, hessian and grain bags.

31

A TALE OF TEAK

In the forests of the deep and acid sands of the Western Province, and especially in the Sesheke and Senanga districts, there grow some of Zambia's most valuable trees. These are *Baikiaea plurijuga*, better known as Zambian teak or Zambesi redwood – trees with strong, straight trunks rising 25m or more from the forest floor and bearing a heavy, rounded crown. Their wood is hard, heavy, strong and durable, with a fine, even texture. It has been used to make railway sleepers, mining timber, doors and furniture, for the white ant cannot eat it; but its hard-wearing quality and handsome appearance have made it most valued as flooring timber. By these uses, the forests have been much diminished in the last 80 years, and the chief agents of this change were Zambesi Saw Mills Limited, which obtained their concession in 1916 and were thus one of the country's first industries.

As timber near Livingstone was cut out and the logging moved further afield, a transport problem arose. This was at first solved by bringing the logs down the Zambesi in barges to a point 15km from the sawmill, and here they were transferred to ox-wagons running on wooden rails. This proved so slow that the company bought steam traction engines with bogies which ran on the rails and driving wheels outside them. By 1924, the company was prospering, and rising output had moved the logging camps too far from the river to make practical use of it. At much the same time, both South African and Rhodesia Railways were changing over from steel to wooden sleepers. Zambesi teak was the best-suited timber in Africa for this purpose, and Zambesi Saw Mills was assured of a long-term future.

But the strength and density of *Baikiaea plurijuga* comes from slow growth: it may take 100 or 140 years to reach a size at which it can be profitably cut. Once exploited, the forest needs 60–70 years to recover. The answer was to move the sawmill into the heart of the forest at Mulobezi and to build a railway connecting it with Livingstone, 180km away. Later, a further 110km of line was added to connect Mulobezi with

76

the logging camp at Kataba. Such a development needed economy of means. The search for it ended at a point 65 years in the past. In 1859–61, South Africa built its first railway, a line running from Cape Town to Wellington, using lightweight, old-fashioned wrought iron rails. When increasing traffic demanded heavier rails, the lightweights were sold to the Bechuanaland Railway Co. which used them until 1903, when some of them were used for the new Gwelo-Umvuma line in Southern Rhodesia. In 1924, they were again found too light for the traffic – and northward they went to replace the wooden rails of the Zambesi Saw Mills Railway, there to complete a century and more of useful service.

The locomotives were not quite so old: the oldest, a Class 7 Neilson 4-8-0 was built in 1892. (In 1967, the wildlife artist and railway enthusiast David Shepherd made the Neilson the hero of his film "Last Train to Mulobezi" – the tale of how he shipped it to Britain.) By 1964, the Sawmills Railway had expanded from one to 18 ancient locomotives, with specimens from 1901 and 1903, and the initial stock of 25 "German Shorts", four-wheel goods wagons of 1922 vintage, had also greatly expanded. The journey from Livingstone to Kataba, with stops for water every 30km, took 15 hours and for many years one train in each direction ran six days a week. But time and economic hardship have taken their toll of the Sawmills (which became part of Indeco in 1968) and its railway, and much has changed.

Today, opposite Livingstone's mainline railway station stands one of ZSR's ancient locomotives on a length of track going nowhere. It marks the entrance to the Zambesi Sawmills Locomotive Sheds National Monument – known more briefly as the Railway Museum, proudly considered by the National Monuments Commission, which opened it on 23 October 1986, as its most ambitious project.

32

THE BIG TREE

Generations of travellers between Ndola and Kitwe are very familiar with the tall tree on the road at Chichele – indeed it is so famous that in 1976 it was declared a National Monument. It is about 160 years old and is a good specimen of mofu or mofwe, known to science as *Entandrophragma delevoyi*. It is about 30m tall and 4m in girth: specimens in less prominent positions have reached up to 40m in height, the tallest trees in Zambia. About 1950, the Commissioner of Forests, Colin Duff, realised that in its prominent position on the busiest road in Zambia it could usefully publicise the value of the country's trees. He placed on it a translation of a Portuguese poem, "The Wayside Tree":

> You who pass by
> And would raise your hand against me,
> Hearken ere you harm me.
> I am your fire on the cold winter nights,
> The friendly shade screening you from the summer sun.
> My fruits quench your thirst on your journey.
> I am the beam that holds up your house,
> The board of your table,
> The bed on which you lie,
> The timber that builds your boat.
> I am the handle of your hoe
> The door of your house,
> The wood of your cradle,
> The shell of your coffin.
> You who pass by
> Hearken to my prayer
> – Harm me not.

The mofu is found in the good rainfall areas of Zambia. It likes deep soil with plenty of shrubs and shade and often grows in family groups,

78

The Big Tree in the 1950s. "You who pass by, hearken to my prayer – harm me not..."

providing oases of pleasant shade. The silver-grey bark of the tall, straight stem and the evergreen, full crown, beckons to travellers as a place of peace. Its red-brown heartwood is proof against the white ant, and it used not to be cut for timber except for making canoes, for which it is considered the best. It is a sacred tree, not to be touched without ceremony. In the First World War, big specimens were sought with great diligence to make the hundreds of canoes used on the river route from Ndola to the Chambeshi to supply the troops on the northern border. In the best practice of canoe making, the tree is not felled, but grubbed up by the roots, a long, hard job. When the tree is down, it is flattened off for a third of its depth and pointed at each end like a pencil; then it is turned over and flattened down another quarter. This is hollowed out to become a fast and serviceable canoe.

Mofu is also considered to provide good medicines. A liquid made from its bark can be used as a drink or rubbed on the body as a tonic, and the leaves smoked as tobacco to relieve asthma. One of the reasons for declaring the tree at Chichele as a monument was because so many medicine seekers were taking its bark that its life was in danger.

33

THE NYIKA PLATEAU

*M*ost of Zambia is on a plateau about 900m above sea level, and most of it is covered by the vast woodland which stretches from Zaire to Zimbabwe and across Africa from Angola to Mozambique – one of the largest areas of the world with a single type of vegetation. In the north-east corner of Zambia, however, on the border with Malawi, the flat woodlands give way to sharply rising hills – part of the vast upheaval which formed the Rift Valley system. From the Mafinga Mountains in the north, the high land runs 100km to the south and to Zambia's tiny section of the Nyika Plateau, at 80sq km the second smallest of her National Parks, and best approached from the much larger Malawi sector.

On the plateau, the peaks of the hills rise above 2 400m, and the woodland gives way to rolling grasslands with patches of ancient forest in the folds. And although the rainfall is not very high – about 1 000mm a year – the altitude ensures cloud and mist throughout the dry season so that it is well watered all year round. It is also cold even in October, and raincoats and warm clothes are essential.

The altitude gives the area a lonely beauty, and Graham Williamson, a well-travelled orchid collector, has called it not only "a naturalist's paradise", but one of the most beautiful places in southern Africa. It has over 100 species of orchid alone, and many other wild flowers. It is rich in small mammals, and is home to many varieties of antelope, to a wide variety of birds, and to some butterflies unique to the patches of forest.

34

THE COPPER FLOWER

*I*n October 1949, a former geologist in Northern Rhodesia, Annan Cook, cabled from the United States to the general manager of the Roan Antelope Mine. "Would be glad," he asked, "if you would cable us the name of the small blue flower associated with copper outcrops. Do you know if a description has been published?" No-one knew, and the unanswered question set in motion search and research which led to the discovery of a valuable indicator of the presence of copper. The vegetation of Zambia includes a number of plants which indicate the presence of minerals, but the "copper flower" is the most interesting.

The research carried out at Luanshya found first of all that there were two very similar plants, both of them about 45cm tall, both having a small, mauvish-white flower. One of them, now known by the scientific name of *Becium obovatum E.Mey*, grows almost anywhere, but the other seemed faithfully to follow the outline of Luanshya's copper deposits. Samples of them were sent to the Curator of Tropical Botany at Kew Gardens in London, where the true copper flower was identified and eventually classified as *Becium homblei de Wild*. Authorities both at Kew and in the botanic garden at Brussels confirmed that no link betwen the flower and copper mineralisation had been known to exist before. They found that it can contain more than 1 000 parts of copper per million, and the roots up to 4 000 parts. The normal copper content of plants found in areas where there is no copper is less than 20 parts per million.

When maps were drawn up showing where *B.homblei* grow, it was found that they coincided accurately with the outcrops of some of the Copperbelt orebodies. However, while the flower will only grow where there is copper, the reverse is not true: some orebodies do not have the copper flower growing on them, and a search for *B.homblei* can never replace conventional prospecting techniques. But it is certainly recorded that it led to the discovery of large reserves of copper ore in an area of the Copperbelt which had been twice covered by prospecting parties in the past.

TALES OF MINES AND MINING

35

WHERE THE COPPER CAME FROM

*T*he Copperbelt mineralisations are estimated by geologists to be somewhere between 600 and 1 000 million years old. The generally accepted outline of the Copperbelt's geological history begins with mountainous country covering much of Zambia, Angola, Zaire and Zimbabwe. Over many millions of years, the mountains were eroded and the ocean came in from the west. Muddy streams from the mountains carried down to the sea not only gravel, sands and clay, but mineral salts in solution. In the shallow coastal lagoons and estuaries, decaying primitive plant and animal life produced sulphuretted hydrogen which in turn precipitated copper, cobalt, nickel and iron minerals in the form of sulphides. As the oceans advanced and the sedimentary basins sank, the copper-bearing formations became covered with great thicknesses of sand, salt and carbonate elements. As millions more years passed, the climate changed. Glaciers came down from the north, carrying boulders from the distant mountains. Primitive plant and animals life flourished in the cold seas, and the shales above and below the glacial deposits found on the Copperbelt today are commonly black with organic carbon.

Then the climate warmed again, the ice melted, more sediments were carried down in the mountain streams and deposited until the accumulation of carbonates, shales and sandstones was three kilometres thick. The basin then began to be lifted up, and the sediments buckled and folded. The old land mass to the south-east moved towards the mountain ridges to the north, and the basin between them was squeezed and folded. Molten rock from deep within the earth's crust squirted up here and there: some of the metallic deposits were dissolved and redeposited. When the folding stopped, weathering and erosion continued until about 250 million years ago, when a second Ice Age brought more glaciers to grind still more of the rocks off the surface and to carry them to the Gwembe Valley, the southern parts of Zimbabwe and even into South Africa. The ice melted: the country became a dry, flat desert.

Then – fortunately for the prospectors of the far distant future – this part of the continent was uplifted nearly 1 000m. The climate became warmer, a blanket of laterite formed over huge areas, obscuring nearly all underlying formations except where an occasional stream broke through. It was along these streams that the rare, copper-stained rocks were noticed by Zambians. Trenching and pitting along these outcrops revealed only low-grade oxide mineralisation which persists to a depth of about 50m, where there is a change from leached secondary oxide to primary sulphide mineralisation commonly extending for several kilometres.

By the 1920s, when the vast sulphide deposits of the Copperbelt were first discovered, the world's consumption of copper was rising fast, and most of the richest and most accessible deposits had been exhausted. The search moved further and further afield, and the average grade of ore declined. Today, most of the world's copper comes from sulphide and oxide minerals irregularly scattered through rock. The world average for ore mined is about 1,5 per cent. The Copperbelt was lucky in having an average grade of about 3,4 per cent.

When the invention and refinement of mechanical equipment made possible the profitable mining of huge amounts of these low-grade ores, it left the problem of treating them since heat alone – the conventional blast furnace used for very high-grade ores – could not deal with a few particles of mineral scattered in huge amounts of barren rock. The first methods of crushing and separating the mineral particles used gravity, but the process used all over the world today is flotation. This depends on the principle that the particles of certain minerals are less easily wetted than those of the host rock. By grinding the ore to a fine powder and stirring it up in a suitable fluid, the minerals can be attached to air bubbles and floated off, while the wet grains of useless rock sink to the bottom.

It was only in 1924, two years before the discovery of the orebody at Luanshya, that the flotation process was perfected by the use of xanthates. These were discovered in 1822, but remained a scientific curiosity for a century, and then sprang suddenly to life in the manufacture of artificial silk, the vulcanisation of rubber – and the separation of copper sulphide minerals from the host rock.

By separation, the minerals are sufficiently concentrated for them to be successfully turned by fire into the red metal so central to Zambia's history.

36

THE FIRST MINERS

Copper was the first metal used by man in any quantity. Although it nearly always appears as a mineral, in a few places it has been found in its metallic form – including in the Copperbelt – and this "native copper" was probably fashioned into implements in Stone Age times. Later, native copper was melted and cast into shapes. The third and most important stage in the development of copper usage came comparatively recently – the conversion of minerals into metal by smelting. The discovery was probably accidental – perhaps the melting of a copper-rich hearthstone. Through excavations in Israel, it is now known that mining and smelting of copper minerals began at least 6 000 years ago. Copper had both practical and decorative uses – on the one hand nails, pipes, weapons, tools; on the other, ornaments, jewellery and statues.

The Bantu immigrants who, some 1 500 years ago, began to move southwards into what is now Zambia, were not only hunters, but farmers who cultivated millet and kept cattle; they were also skilled in making decorated pottery and in metal working. They used iron for the most part, but other metals such as copper where they found surface deposits. The first written reference to copper mining in south-central Africa originated with a Portuguese traveller in 1591, and its reference to "the mines of Bembe" may possibly have been associated with Lake Bangweulu and the Bemba people. But it seems to have been the growth of the superior social, economic and political organisation of the builders of Zimbabwe in the 16th century that sparked the growth of the copper trade in what is now the Shaba province of Zaire in the north and the Transvaal in the south. By the middle decades of the 19th century, the Zimbabwe empire had long perished, but copper was being traded as far north as Uganda and by the Arab slavers to the east and west coasts. Livingstone met a caravan in 1868 with slaves carrying five tonnes of copper.

By the time the first white prospectors had come to Zambia and Zaire in the closing years of the 19th century, however, the Arab influence, and its indigenous mining, had declined almost to vanishing point, but

It is thought that the old-time miners of Shaba Province in Zaire produced at least 100 000 tonnes of copper, breaking hard rock with fire and water, digging out the richest ore with iron picks, hauling it up shafts as deep as 30m in bark buckets.

Africans were still mining and smelting copper, and their methods have not to this day been lost. Only the richest malachite ores were used, and were mined usually from circular shafts 10–15m deep, but which, in very firm ground, went down as much as 30m. Deep trenches such as those found at Kansanshi and Bwana Mkubwa were also used. In Shaba, an ancient working was recorded at over 1 000m in length and between 200 and 300m wide. It has been calculated that in Shaba alone, prehistoric mining produced at least 100 000 tonnes of copper, requiring the removal of over a million tonnes of ore and waste.

Mining was carried out by digging the softer rocks with iron-headed picks and by breaking hard rock with fire and water. Ore and waste were hauled out in bark buckets. Smelting sites were often some distance away near water and anthills from which to draw refractory material to build furnaces. The fuel used was charcoal made from hardwood, and the draught was produced with skin bellows whose nozzle was cemented with mud into a clay tuyere or blast pipe. In Africa as elsewhere in ancient times, the process of smelting was surrounded with magic and religious ceremony. A Belgian missionary described the scene at the climax of the work and ritual: "It is eleven o'clock at night, the fire splutters in the furnaces. It is a luminous oasis, frenzied in the heart of the silent forest which sleeps under a limpid sky, deep and brilliant with stars. Soon the flames change, a plume of blue and green, brightening into gold, crowns the furnace and throws sharp lights on the ebony bodies. The green malachite begins to melt and to trickle down in shining rivulets into the fire; and that is the great moment, for stones are not things which melt, and it is the Spirits of the Mountain who are showing their power by this miracle. The rhythm of the clapping quickens and the great song swells until it echoes in the gaping hills … In half an hour the process is complete; strong men bring branches and break the furnace down, and there in a hollow at the bottom lies the molten copper." A more prosaic record of primitive mining and smelting was made in the 1920s by a Copperbelt and Katanga pioneer, Raymond Brooks and his colleague R.R. Sharp with photographs of each stage of the process. As recently as 1962, Ndola Copper Refineries' stand at the Ndola show featured daily demonstrations of their ancient craft by three old men from Kansanshi, where archaeologists have found evidence of four distinct cultural groups who mined and smelted malachite there between the 4th and 19th centuries.

In ancient times, mining was continuous through the dry season with men, women and children helping and the miners and their families living in temporary grass shelters until it was time to sow the next season's food crop. There were often many furnaces used at a single smelting, each of them charged with about 50kg of ore yielding 10 to 15kg of copper. The solidified metal was then taken to smaller furnaces in which it was refined by a further melting and then poured into moulds, usually of clay, but sometimes made of soapstone. The copper was moulded in the shape of a capital I, a St. Andrew's cross, or a capital H. These crosses and bars, which weighed from 10 to 50kg, were used as a currency throughout south-central Africa. Copper was also traded as wire made by drawing hot metal through a hole in a crucible-shaped draw plate. Wire, or a flattened ribbon of copper, was used for weapons, for bullets, for ceremonial purposes, and for inlaying ironwork. The ancients' methods were simple but effective, and they achieved some remarkable results. For over 30 years, European prospectors directed their efforts almost exclusively towards the "discovery" of ancient workings, and the major Copperbelt mines all originated from them. Chibuluma, in 1939, was the first Copperbelt orebody to be discovered by scientific exploration methods.

37

THE STORY OF KABWE MINE

*I*n January 1902, an Australian mining engineer, Tom Davey, was completing a 250km trek east from the Kafue River to check on reports of ancient copper mines at Kitakata when his guide confessed he was lost. Davey pitched his tent in pouring rain while the guide moved off to try to establish their position. He soon came back saying he could take Davey to Kitakata and back before dark. Davey followed him, and while crossing a broad dambo, he saw what appeared to be a brown ironstone kopje. The area was, and is, known to Zambians as Kabwe, the place of smelting, because of its abundant iron ore resources.

Davey found the ancient copper workings insignificant, and made his way back to the kopje. He climbed up it, knocking off with his prospector's hammer pieces of the rock as he passed them. "It was not long before I broke a heavy piece of stone which was perfectly white, and which I at once recognised as cerusite or carbonate of lead …" After five days of excited exploration, Davey named his discovery "The Rhodesia Broken Hill" after a famous mine with similarly mixed ores of lead and zinc in his native Australia.

Indeed, Kabwe mine, as its name became nearly 80 years later, had the most complex and interesting mineralisation in all Zambia, and it has been said that no mine in the world produced more beautiful specimens from some 25 different minerals of lead, zinc, vanadium and copper. Nowhere else in Zambia have such significant deposits of lead and zinc been found. Quarrying of high-grade zinc ore began in 1904 as the railway moved north from Livingstone, and on its arrival in 1906, exports of crudely-treated ore were shipped to Swansea. In the succeeding years, the mine had many technical and financial difficulties, and by 1932 the easily mined and treated ores were approaching exhaustion. When Sir Edmund Davis, chairman of the board of directors of the mine, was touring Northern Rhodesia in his private railway carriage in 1934, he told the geologist Dr Joseph Bancroft that Broken Hill had never been a payable venture, and he had only refrained from closing it down because "it would disperse a happy town." Now the world was beginning to recover from the Great Depression, and Bancroft persuaded Davis that beneath the opencast workings there were large tonnages of profitable ore.

Shafts were sunk to exploit them and mining from them began in 1938. By 1960, Broken Hill had in its 56 years of life produced 315 000 tonnes of lead and 625 000 tonnes of zinc. But by the 1990s, Kabwe was losing money, and running out of ore. In April 1994, Government and the operators, the nationalised company Zambia Consolidated Copper Mines, agreed that it should be closed on 30 June and offered for sale, just 90 years after the first ore was quarried from Tom Davey's kopje.

The mine may in time be forgotten by the outside world, but it has an honoured place in the history of the evolution of mankind. In June 1907, a cavern was exposed at the western end of the kopje orebody which became known as "the bone cave." Within this cavity there was an amazing accumulation of bones more or less cemented by oxide lead and zinc minerals. Bones, teeth and horn cores of the larger antelopes were most common, but there were also the remains of elephant, hippopotamus, rhinoceros, giraffe, leopard, birds and rodents, a few human bones and some stone implements. In June 1921, there was a far more important discovery. Blasting about 30m below the surface revealed another cave and – miraculously untouched by the explosion – there on a ledge was a human skull. After being exposed for some days on top of a pole, the possible value of the skull was recognised by the mine doctor, and the mine manager, R.K. McCartney, took it personally to the British Museum in September 1921, where Sir Arthur Smith Woodward, the Keeper of Geology, gave it the name of *Homo rhodesiensis*, Rhodesian man. His skull is thought to have been in the cave for up to 30 000 years. There is a hole in it which was probably made by a pointed wooden spear – an early example of human conflict.

38

THE TALE OF THE ROAN ANTELOPE

*M*ining is one of the most dramatic of industries, and from all over the world there are stories of chance discoveries that lead to great mines. Zambia has a good share of these romantic tales, and the most famous of them is the story of the roan antelope. It happened in 1902, a vital year in Zambian economic history. The hero of the story is Bill Collier, and over many years his telling of the tale varied in detail, but not in its important aspects.

William Collier was born in England in 1870, and sailed for South Africa when he was 18. For the next 14 years he moved around working as a prison warder, as a policeman in Bechuanaland and a gold prospector in Southern Rhodesia. In 1902, he and another prospector, J.J. O'Donoghue, were summoned from Bulwayo by Tom Davey, consulting engineer and senior director to the Northern Copper (BSA) Co. A few weeks earlier, he had discovered the lead and zinc deposits he had called Broken Hill, and he was now hot on the trail of more minerals. Davey sent them to the area of what are now Ndola and Luanshya and to look for signs of ancient copper workings. They soon found the local people were accustomed to using powdered malachite as a dressing for tropical ulcers: it was a promising sign, and to cover the ground more quickly, they split up.

As he walked the bush, asking people if they had seen any signs of mining or of minerals, an old man, seeing Collier's gun, asked him to shoot some meat. Collier obliged, and in return, the old man directed Bill to the area of the Luanshya stream. Here in a clearing it happened that a roan antelope bull presented him with a clear shot. It fell on a patch of dark grey shale in which Bill's practised eye quickly picked out the green of malachite in knife-blade seams. Nearby, as the old man had promised, there were signs of ancient workings.

Next day, on a careful exploration, Collier traced a long, narrow U-

Bill Collier shot a roan antelope and started the Copperbelt...With an irony he probably did not enjoy, one of Collier's last jobs was as caretaker at the then developing mine, Nchanga, when it was closed by flooding and the world depression in 1931.

shaped clearing a kilometre in length, its arms a few hundred metres apart. To an experienced prospector, the lack of vegetation was a clear indication of the presence of minerals. He pegged 50 claims on one arm calling it Roan Antelope, and 20 on the other, calling it Rietbok (Reedbuck). The discovery was followed up by some trenching, but it was abandoned in favour of what then seemed to be the more promising deposits at Bwana Mkubwa to which he and O'Donoghue were led on 4 December 1902. It was not until 1925 that a young American engineer, Russell J. Parker, came to examine the long arms of the Roan and Rietbok claims. After more trenching and digging of shafts to greater depth, Parker came to a dramatic conclusion: the Roan and Rietbok arms were the top of a syncline – a huge U of mineralised rock plunging deep into the ground, where the thin oxide copper minerals at the surface changed to rich sulphides. In April 1926, William Selkirk, a crusty old pioneer of prospecting in Central Africa, and now consulting engineer and senior director of the mining company Selection Trust, came to see the evidence for himself. He confirmed Parker's opinion, and decided the deposit was likely to be large and uniform. Accordingly, Selkirk recommended a daringly economical programme of drilling at 300m intervals. Clean sulphide ore in an 11m belt, assaying at 3,87 per cent copper was intersected at 150m – and the Copperbelt was born. The orebody proved to be in the shape of an enormous ship's hull, with a keel 11km long and in places a kilometre deep. Roan Antelope Copper Mines Ltd was incorporated on 3 June 1927, and the first copper was cast in the smelter on 23 October 1931. The mine kept its romantic name until 1964, when it took the name of the Luanshya stream. By then it had produced over two million tonnes of copper.

And Bill Collier? He went back to England, married his wife Jessie, and returned to Africa, working in what are now Zimbabwe, Zaire and Zambia. From the middle 1920s he lived and worked in modest jobs on the Copperbelt and watched it grow until 1935 when, now 65, his health began to fail. The Roan Antelope company, in recognition of his discovery, granted him an annuity. He retired to Dorset in England where he died in 1943. Jessie followed him in 1954. In 1960, Sir Ronald Prain, chairman of the then RST Group of mining companies, unveiled the Collier monument at the mine. It is not at the exact spot where Bill shot the roan antelope, for that is now in a caved, mined-out area, but 200m away on undisturbed ground.

39

SANGUNI, THE LUANSHYA SNAKE

In 1927, when work started on developing Roan Antelope, the first of the Copperbelt mines, the most serious problem the company had to deal with was the legend of Sanguni, the great, many-headed snake which lived in the Luanshya stream. Stories abounded of the shape and size of the Snake, its colour, activities, methods of killing, frequency of visits to particular points of the river, and the reasons for its visits and the killings took as many forms as the imagination could conjure up. Recruitment of workers from villages for miles around was almost impossible. "No," they would say, "we cannot go to work at that place because that is where the Snake dwells." Any death or accident at the mine was counted another victim of the Snake, and deserters spread the story further afield. When a surveyor's assistant disappeared from the river bank, the story seemed to be fully confirmed.

The mine management was well aware of the dangers of malaria, dysentery and many other diseases among the employees in what was clearly a seriously unhealthy area, shunned by the local people – and perhaps this was the origin of the tale of the death-dealing snake. As far away as Cape Town, intending travellers to the Copperbelt were jocularly told not to bother to buy a return ticket … Then, by good fortune, "Chirupula" Stephenson, the man who came to the Lala country in 1900, who was magistrate at Ndola in 1904, and who was married to the daughter of a Lala chief, called on his old district to see the dramatic changes the past 20 years had brought. Dave Irwin, the American general manager of Roan Antelope, saw a golden opportunity. Would Chirupula use his prestige to arrange a ceremony of exorcism to remove from the river the dreaded Snake?

Chirupula was flattered and delighted. He sought out a senior chief of the Lamba, who in turn sought out his uncle, the aged Chief Katanga, the priest-king, who alone could offer up prayers of supplication, and his sister Chalwe. As many chiefs and sons of chiefs as could be found were gathered, a spirit hut was built, a white rooster was killed, meal was sprinkled. Katanga and Chalwe performed a slow, stately dance. An ox was killed, much beer was drunk. The Snake was exorcised – though the Bemba were not convinced. "With all tribes represented there and each calling upon his forefathers' spirits", they said, "with so many different tribes, how do we know that some of those spirits were not long ago enemies to each other, and being enemies, how can we expect anything but trouble now?"

But Sanguni was indeed exorcised, not by prayers, but by the public health campaign carried out by the Ross Institute – named after the man who discovered the link between mosquitoes and malaria. It was one of the greatest – and most successful – mosquito eradication campaigns ever carried out. It included canalisation of the Luanshya stream. Its level was lowered; its many twists and turns were straightened, and its dark, stagnant pools were drained. Ah, said the people, Sanguni has had to leave Luanshya to find deeper waters elsewhere; and the fear of the Snake at last died away.

40

THE PRINCE AND THE POWER STATION

When Edward Prince of Wales – later, and briefly, King Edward VIII – made a tour of Southern Africa in 1925, the most northerly point of his journey from Cape Town was Broken Hill, the oldest operating mine in Northern Rhodesia. The purpose of his visit, on 15 July 1925, was to open the Mulungushi scheme – the dam which feeds the hydro-electric power station built 34 years before Kariba produced its first electricity in 1959. The huge zinc silicate deposits of the Broken Hill mine were known in the mine's early days, but the problems of extracting the metal by leaching and electrowinning were for long unsolved. It was not until 1924 that Royale Stevens, the American chief metallurgist at the mine, built a successful pilot plant to produce electrolytic zinc. The new process needed large amounts of cheap electricity. As early as 1901, the pioneer prospector Frank Lewis had recorded the hydro-electric potential of the Mulungushi Falls 60km east-south-east of the mine. The time had come to exploit this good fortune.

A dam was built across a narrow gorge where the Mulungushi River passes through a rocky ridge 10km above the falls, forming a reservoir 25km long by 7km wide. Water from the dam was diverted to a steel pipe running 377m down to the power station. The coincidence of its completion with the arrival in Northern Rhodesia of the Prince of Wales was an opportunity not to be missed, and his tour was happily extended to Broken Hill and Mulungushi. It was from what G. Ward Price, then one of Britain's best-known foreign correspondents, described as "a whole village of picturesque pavilions" high above the power station, that the Prince officially opened the scheme and stayed for an elaborate luncheon whose every dish had been brought by train from Johannesburg, 1 600km to the south. A silver medal was cast to commemorate the occasion; when one came on the London market in the 1990s, it fetched £220.

The leaching and electrowinning plant was opened in 1928. In 1945, just 20 years after the Prince's visit, a second and bigger hydro-electric station was built on the Lunsemfwa River, 90km from Kabwe, followed in 1958 by a huge dam in the Mita Hills, 20km upstream from the power station, to enable it to run at full capacity all the year round.

41

How We Lost Katanga

*B*etween the mid-16th century and the end of the 19th century, it has been estimated that pre-European copper smelters had extracted at least 100 000 tonnes from the rich oxide ores of the Katanga area of Central Africa. Rumours and travellers' tales had long told of its wealth. When the European Powers met at the Berlin Conference of 1885, Katanga was included in the claim of King Leopold of the Belgians to a million square miles of what he called "the Congo Independent State", with himself as its sovereign and despot. Leopold by that time was dealing with what he considered more urgent matters, and after several years of practical inaction, the idea was put forward in the British press that unoccupied parts of the Congo State could be taken over by anyone who chose to occupy them effectively.

In 1889, Cecil Rhodes formed the British South Africa Company, and his territorial ambitions knew no limits. In February 1892, a Belgian professor of geology, Dr. Jules Cornet, accompanied an expedition to Katanga and sent the first specimens of its copper ore to Europe. But he had neither the experience nor the equipment to make a proper assessment of the value of the vast number of ancient workings he saw, and reported that their low value and distance from the sea put aside any idea of exploitation at least for the present. But a map of Katanga was prepared despite the lack of detailed knowledge of it. Rhodes decided to put to the test the old adage that possession is nine points of the law. If he could make a treaty with Msiri, the ruler of the area, and make British possession valid by all the outward signs of occupation, it would have to be recognised under the terms of the Berlin confererncE.

Although the BSA Company was somewhat overstretched at this time – and the British Foreign Office severely disapproving – Rhodes sent his emissary Alfred Sharpe in 1890 to get Msiri to sign a treaty. Msiri was described by Harry Johnston as "a stranger to the country of Katanga, being merely a Mnyamwezi slave trader who, by the aid of an armed rabble of Wanyamwezi freebooters and coast Arabs, had carved out a kingdom for himself. He was a persistent slave raider, and was hated by the people over whom he ruled ..." The pioneer missionary Fred Arnot, who described Msiri at this time as "an old-looking man with a pleasant-smooth face, and a short beard, quite white," warned Msiri not to sign his country away. When Sharpe arrived, Msiri furiously dismissed him.

The Belgians not surprisingly decided they should quickly reinforce their claim by winning Msiri over to a treaty with them and establishing their authority over his kingdom. Captain William Stairs, a young Canadian serving in the British army who had experience of African exploration with Stanley, was given leave to lead an expedition financed by the Katanga Company, an international syndicate with mineral rights which had much in common with Rhodes's BSA Company. His second-in-command was a Belgian officer, Capt. Bodson, and the party which set out from Dar es Salaam in June 1891 included a doctor, Joseph Moloney, and a caravan of 336 askari and porters. They reached Msiri's capital, Bunkeya, on 14 December after five months and ten days, with 120 marches averaging 13km a day. Here were ivory, salt, slaves, copper and iron to trade; here on his palisades and on the trees, skulls were hung like hats on pegs, on every available arm – the skulls of his enemies and of his subjects alike. His harem of women numbered some five hundred.

Msiri himself, wrote Dr. Moloney in his published account of the affair, was dressed in a silk cloak covered with gold lace, a pair of trousers and huge jack-boots. After several inconclusive days of talks and prevarications, Stairs, exasperated, told Msiri he would hoist the Congo State flag "whether you desire it or not." Msiri's answer was to leave under cover of darkness for Munema, a fortified village a short distance away. A strong party under Capt. Bodson was sent to arrest him the next morning. Bodson called on Msiri to surrender to Stairs. Msiri looked angered. He said nothing, but laid his hand on his sword – a gift from Stairs. Bodson at once shot him dead. One of Msiri's men shot Bodson in the stomach, a wound from which he died that night.

Msiri was buried without incident, his followers dispersed and his empire distributed among the chiefs. Stairs supervised the hoisting of the Congo Free State's blue flag with its yellow star, and, by the end of January, they had completed the laborious building of a mud and timber stockade that Stairs christened Fort Bunkeya. But these were the hunger months: supplies were running short, there was no food to be bartered, and disease, starvation and death were increasing among the party. Stairs had a second attack of blackwater, and the other whites, except Dr. Moloney, were themselves half-dead from fever. Among the carriers, eleven died in a week. The expedition subsisted on a diet of cooked leaves and grass, on locusts and fried white ants. "Their nastiness passes my power of description," wrote Moloney. The rains poured down and fever increased.

As soon as they were relieved by a Belgian party in February, they set off on the long, arduous, fever-ridden journey to Lake Nyasa, the Shire, the Zambesi, and the sea. It was 5 July when they sailed for Zanzibar and England from Chinde – just too late for Stairs, who died there, within sound of the surf, from his last attack of blackwater.

Thanks to him, Katanga was safe in the hands of the Belgians and of the Zaireans of the future, with a copper industry that would become second in Africa only to that of Zambia. Robert Williams, an associate of Rhodes, had long believed in the mineral wealth of the Congo-Zambesi divide, and in 1899, George Grey, working for Williams's Tanganyika Concessions, went into Katanga and saw the low, treeless hills with their green copper oxide outcrops giving a brilliant visual display. By 1906, when the Union Miniere du Haut Katanga was formed to mine them, over 100 significant copper deposits had been marked. "In the known history of mining," wrote the distinguished geologist Joseph Bancroft, "no similar area has been found in which so many important exposures of copper ores have been recorded in so short a time." It was thanks to Williams and the riches of Katanga that the money was raised to take the railway from Broken Hill to Sakania in the Congo by 1909, and to complete the railway from Benguela to the Congo border in 1928.

42

THE MINE THAT NEARLY DIED

At five minutes to three on the morning of 25 September 1970, the lights went out underground at Mufulira. All power failed, and a gale of foul air blasted through the darkened workings of the mine. Then, with a great noise, began the worst disaster ever suffered by the Zambian mining industry. Within 15 minutes, over a million tonnes of mud and water had squirted under terrifying, irresistible pressure throughout a large part of the country's biggest underground mine. On the surface, at No. 3 Tailings Dam, a huge funnel-shaped depression rapidly formed.

Underground, there were 461 men on night-shift. Almost before silence returned and the first shocked survivors began to emerge, rescue teams were alerted and the long-practised drills began. Gallons of strong-smelling eucalyptus oil were poured down the ventilation shafts as a silent signal to evacuate the mine. Within 50 minutes, the first rescue team was 500m underground and moving into a situation that was unknown – except that it contained terrible dangers.

Already other rescue teams were racing across the Copperbelt to Mufulira, and soon every accessible part of the mine had been examined. The magnitude of the disaster was clear, and there were two concurrent crises: first to rescue whoever might have survived, and second to save the mine. None of the deep-level pump stations was working and water was entering the mine at thousands of cubic metres an hour. If it was not stopped, there would be no rescues, and probably no mine.

For six days, the rescue teams tirelessly laboured underground, crawling, wading, even swimming – knowing each minute that a further inrush from above could engulf them without hope of survival. They searched every part of the mine not inundated by mud, and rescued four men who otherwise would have died. They found none of the dead: all of them were buried in the mud, the results of whose violence and fury they now witnessed. Over a depth of 600m, thousands of metres of tunnels were choked. Huge pieces of equipment had been flung like toys, crushers and conveyors buried, pipes and cables ripped out. And 89 men were missing. On surface, it was known that water was rising in the mine at the rate of 200mm a minute. A project office was opened to obtain pumps, motors, cables, pipes from around the Copperbelt. Underground, 400 men worked 12-hour shifts to instal an emergency pumping system. They did three months' work in seven days in conditions of appalling strain and difficulty.

On Sunday 4 October, the water stopped rising. Two weeks later, one pump developed a fault, another being lowered down a shaft slipped and damaged two more; pumping was halved and the mine began to flood again. An exhausting battle was fought for eleven days before control was restored. And between the overriding urgencies of the search for survivors and the saving of the mine, there was a third: to find out what had happened and why.

The seeds of the accident were planted in the 1930s, nearly 40 years before, in Mufulira's early days, when waste material from the concentrator was used to fill hollows in which malaria-carrying mosquitoes could breed. Then, when a new mining method was introduced in 1946, large-scale subsidence began to appear on the surface above the mined area, causing the appearance of two large ponds every rain season. It was decided to use the fine sands, or tailings, from the concentrator to fill the ponds and grade them so that rainwater ran off.

President Kaunda at the dedication of the memorial to the 89 men who died in the Mufulira disaster.

There was a further change in mining methods in 1966 which caused further subsidence. No-one realised that this movement was affecting the under-side of the huge blanket of fine sand. Dry, it was inert and harmless. Saturated with rainwater, it behaved like a fluid, dangerous and unpredictable. On that terrible night in September 1970, suddenly, beneath the blanket of sand and water there formed an open chimney into the mine through which the flood poured under unimaginable pressure through a gigantic funnel.

Saving the mine and restoring it to full production took four years of unremitting toil – clearing out thousands of tonnes of mud, sealing off the danger areas, hauling away a million tonnes of waste rock from a dump overlooking and threatening the sinkhole, stabilising the tailings dump with 600 tube wells, and scores of similar projects to save the life of a great mine. Not the least of them was the preservation of the morale among 9 000 employees and maintaining their confidence that Mufulira would win through. The last chapter was completed in 1976, when President Kaunda unveiled a monument in a memorial garden for the 89 men who died in the mud and darkness of that black day in September 1970.

43

BURNING THE BUSH

When the first three big Copperbelt mines were developed before the Second World War, each one had its own power station burning coal imported by rail from Southern Rhodesia. At the end of the war, however, the pace of development in both countries was so fast that the colliery at Wankie could not produce enough coal for their needs – and the railways were so overloaded they could not have distributed it. Imports from South Africa, and even from the United States, on the Benguela Railway, were still failing to bridge the gap, and the Copperbelt faced huge losses through inability to generate all the power needed to mine, smelt and refine 300 000 tonnes of copper a year.

In 1947, managements of the two mining companies – Rhodesian Selection Trust and the Anglo American Corporation – met to discuss the rapidly worsening crisis. They agreed that a high voltage network controlled from Kitwe, linking all their power stations together, would give greatly improved efficiency and flexibility. But it would take two years, and it would reduce, but not end, the coal shortage. What was to be done? The answer stood all about them – the vast forests of the Copperbelt. They would burn the bush to make electricity. It was an enormous undertaking. About 25 firms were sub-contracted for the cutting, which began late in 1947. In their first few months, they cut over 100 000 tonnes of timber. In 1948 they cut 340 000 tonnes, in 1949 and 1950 600 000 tonnes, and in 1951, 750 000 tonnes. The area cleared each year was about 12 000ha, and it was cleared not with chain saws and sawmills, but by 7 000 men with hand axes. The logs then had to be hauled up to 20km to the mines over the roughest of tracks. It cost two or three times as much as coal, but with the copper price high, it was worth it.

By 1952, 20 of the Copperbelt's 36 power-generating boilers had been converted to run wholly or partly on wood – in itself a considerable feat of engineering – and wood was providing a third to a half of all the power needed to produce the country's copper. It was a programme without known precedent in the world mining industry. Even so, calculations of the growth of mine output showed clearly that there would again be a shortage of power in 1957. By good fortune, the Belgian Congo was building a major hydro-electric plant on the Lualaba River which would have spare capacity: in 1956, a 500km transmission line connected it with Kitwe, and by 1959, the Copperbelt was drawing half its power from Le Marinel. Power consumption was now matching output – there was nothing to spare. But in that same year of 1959, the Copperbelt was connected to Kariba, and the crisis was finally over.

Copperbelt bush takes 30 to 50 years to regenerate, and the wood-cutting could, in theory, have gone on indefinitely. But the distances over which the logs would have to be carried would have become impossible for practical purposes. The story of the great wood-burning has instead become one of the forgotten dramas of Zambia's mining industry.

MEMORIALS TO THE PAST

44

DR. LIVINGSTONE DIED HERE

On 25 August 1872, Dr. Livingstone set out from Unyanyembe, 320km from Ujiji on Lake Tanganyika, on a last vain effort to find the source of the River Nile. He was 59 years old, worn out by illness and endless journeying on foot. He planned to walk to the southern end of Lake Tanganyika, then south-west to Lake Bangweulu and its swamps, then west towards the place he called "the ancient fountains of Katanga." A story he had heard from Arab traders led him to believe that here he would solve one of the last great geographical mysteries. It was not the source of the Nile, however, but the area in which were the sources of the Zambesi, the Kafue and the Lualaba rivers.

By the beginning of 1873, Livingstone, soaked by rain and half-drowned in mud, was also half-lost in the vastness of the Bangweulu Swamps. On 19 March, his sixtieth birthday, he was desperately searching for dry land, and also desperately ill. By 21 April he was too weak to walk; on 25 April he was carried to villagers who knew nothing of the four "ancient fountains." It was the final and most bitter disappointment. On 27 April, he made his last diary entry: "Knocked up quite ..." He was carried gently, for he was in unbearable pain, by his followers, led by the faithful Chuma and Susi, who had been with him for the past seven years, to the village of Chief Chitambo in the country they called Ilala. Majwara, a young boy who was sent to sleep outside Livingstone's hut, came to Susi near dawn. "I am afraid," he said. Susi found Livingstone on his knees by the bed, his head buried in his hands upon the pillow. Now came Chuma and others of the doctor's men, and by the light of a candle they saw he was dead. They covered his body with a cloth, and went out and sat by the fire. A cock crowed: it was the first day of May 1873.

Susi and Chuma feared that if Chitambo learnt the expedition was now leaderless, he might levy a heavy charge upon it, and for a while they prevaricated. But when at last they admitted Livingstone was not ill, but dead, Chitambo told them not to be afraid. "Now my people shall mourn," he said. Drums were beaten for three hours, and the young men fired their guns. The village ballad maker chanted a special dirge: "… An elephant is dead from a spear wound. The lovely one has gone …" Chitambo himself said: "I believe he is a great man." It was resolved that the body, together with Livingstone's diaries, maps and scientific instruments, should be carried to the coast. Farjallah, who had been assistant to Dr. James Christie, physician to the Sultan of Zanzibar, removed Livingstone's heart and internal organs. He found the lower gut closed by a clot of blood the size of a man's fist, the cause of his agonies. These parts were buried deep below the floor of a roofless hut in which the operation was conducted. Jacob Wainwright, a Yao like Chuma, who had some schooling in India, read from the Bible. Then the thin, worn body was covered in salt and left in the sun for two weeks, watched continually by day and candlelight.

Before they left on their long, arduous journey, Wainwright carved an inscription, giving the names of the 'heads of department' on a tree in the enclosure:

Dr. Livingstone
May 4, 1873
Yazuza, Mniasere
Vchopere

With the body shrouded in tarred canvas and wrapped in bark, the party of seventy men and women set off for the coast. Delayed for weeks by illness and the hardships of the journey, it was not until 20 October that Chuma, leading a small advance party, reached Unyanyembe to bring the news of Livingstone's death, and it was February 1874 before the expedition reached Bagamoyo, opposite Zanzibar, crying "Heria bahari!" – "Welcome sea!" They had walked 2 250km in nine months, lost at least ten of their party to disease, but had kept their promise to bring Livingstone's body back to his own people. It has been said, and it is difficult to deny, that it was the most famous, and in some ways the most remarkable journey in African exploration.

Susi and Chuma, never rewarded for their devotion, were brought to England to help edit Livingstone's "Last Journals," too late for them to see the great explorer buried in Westminster Abbey. But they were now famous for their exploits, and for a while were much sought-after caravan leaders in Zanzibar. But neither lived to old age: Chuma died in 1882, aged about 32, Susi in 1891, when he was about 42. The oldest survivor was another Yao, Chengwimbe, called Matthew Wellington, who died in Kenya in 1935 when he was nearly 90.

The Livingstone memorial at Chitambo's village, built in 1902. It shows the bronze cross which replaced the original masonry one, destroyed by a madman who came specially from the Copperbelt in October 1948 with an axe and a crowbar to knock down the top third of the obelisk.

In 1899, Robert Codrington, Administrator of North-Eastern Rhodesia, caused the tree at Chitambo's to be cut down because the inscription was already being damaged by insects, and he had it sent to the Royal Geographical Society in London. It was not until 1902 that funds were raised to build a memorial at the place where Livingstone's heart was buried. An artisan, Owen Stroud, came from Fort Jameson to build a smooth obelisk of bricks he burnt on the spot, topped with a cross, and inscribed with two brass tablets. It is not far from the Great North Road and the Tazara railway, arteries of commerce in the heart of Africa of which Livingstone would have surely approved.

45

THE LAST SHOTS OF WORLD WAR I

On 11 November 1918 – at the eleventh hour of the eleventh day of the eleventh month – the long-drawn out massacres of the First World War ended with the most famous truce in history, the Armistice. In Livingstone, the capital of Northern Rhodesia, Government learnt the news from a Reuter's cable that evening. But far to the north, at the little factory built to process wild rubber, nothing was known either to the Germans advancing on the river, or to the modest British forces defending it. The Germans, under Major-General Paul von Lettow-Vorbeck, conducting a brilliant guerilla-type campaign in Mozambique, had swung west into Northern Rhodesia, occupied Kasama on 9 November, and sent patrols ahead to find a river crossing to continue their raiding, loot-

General Paul von Lettow-Vorbeck

ing and fighting – perhaps to blow up the copper mines of Katanga or to head for the Angolan coast ...

The Germans had long since cut Rhodes's Africa Transcontinental Telegraph Company's line from Salisbury through Nyasaland to Abercorn and on to Ujiji in German East Africa. When the volunteers of the Northern Rhodesia Rifles trekked from Broken Hill to the northern border

Just 35 years after the last shots of the First World War were fired at the Chambeshi river crossing, a memorial was unveiled there on 14 November 1953.

in December 1914, the wagon train carried enough copper wire for a lightweight military telegraph line between Kasama and the line of rail at Kashitu, near Ndola. Two young men, Frank Rushforth and Eric Pullon, led the gangs which strung it with remarkable speed from trees and bush poles. They covered 400 miles in three months – up to 20km a day – and then went from Kasama another 160km to Abercorn to complete the connection between Livingstone and the far northern border.

But despite regular patrols, the elements, the elephants, the popularity of copper wire and ready-pierced porcelain insulators as female decoration, made breakages and failures frequent.

Thus it was, as a historian has noted, "entirely in keeping with the aggressiveness of Von Lettow's army that it should have learned of its own defeat by capturing the news." On 13 November, a German patrol took prisoner a British motor-cyclist carrying despatches to the commander of the forces pursuing them. His name was Herring, and he was the last prisoner taken in the First World War. Among the despatches he carried was the announcement of the Armistice and a message for Von Lettow calling on him to order a cease fire. By this time, his advance patrols had reached the Chambeshi and opened fire on the rubber factory: for a full hour, the small Northern Rhodesian forces fired back. At last, at 11 o'clock in the morning of 13 November, just 48 hours after the guns had fallen silent in Europe, the full message arrived by telegraph at the factory: Germany had agreed to the unconditional surrender of Von Lettow's forces. Half an hour later, a party set out under a white flag to bring the terms to Von Lettow and his men who, cut off for a year from the rest of the world, and still victorious, were appalled to learn the extent of Germany's abject defeat. It was Hector Croad, the magistrate at Kasama, who told Von Lettow the next day of revolution in Germany, mutiny in the Imperial fleet, and the abdication of the Kaiser. Von Lettow agreed to march his command to Abercorn – the nearest source of sufficient food – for a formal surrender of his little, undefeated army: 1 300 soldiers and 1 500 carriers and the women and children who had followed them as they outwitted forces 60 times larger.

On 14 November 1953, exactly 35 years later, a stone monument to the surrender was unveiled at what was then the pontoon crossing of the Chambeshi. It is surmounted by a German field gun sent by the British Government for just this purpose, but which had been stored at Livingstone since 1919. Among those present at its unveiling were 92 ex-askari wearing their medal ribbons, the Paramount Chief Chitimukulu and his councillors, and a guard of honour and the band of the Northern Rhodesia Regiment.

There is a monument to the official surrender at Abercorn as well, to the moment when the askari reluctantly laid down their arms, and the officers, in honour of their gallant army, retained theirs. Paul Von Lettow-Vorbeck, increasingly a hero to his enemies as well as his own people, died in 1964 at the age of 94.

46

THE STATUE OF CHIEF MUKOBELA

*T*n the old days, the Ila people of the Southern Province lived on the flood plains of the Kafue River where there were rich grazing for their cattle and vast herds of every kind of antelope and buffalo. There were plentiful fish in the river, rich soil in which to grow crops. With good food and constant exercise in the swamp-like flats, the people grew tall and strong. "Ndi Mwila," a young man would say, "I am a Mwila," confident in his superiority. All outside their narrow kingdom were Balumbu, barbarians. Young Ila boys had their hair gathered into a cone, impumbe, made with wax and clay. After the rains, before the harvest, the young men had their impumbe transformed into isusu. It is a process which may take a month and in which twine and hair bought from others were stretched and stitched painfully into a fine-pointed cone with a sable antelope horn in its centre. It was as much as a metre in length, and while he wore it, a man's isusu had to be tied at night to the rafters of his hut. It is believed that the origin of this uncomfortable fashion was the need to keep each other in sight while hunting or fighting in the thick cane brakes and reeds of their country. The scornful name "Mashukulumbwe" given to the Ila by their neighbours, the Lozi, means "Those who brush up their hair."

Every year in the old days, when the great herds of buffalo came down from the forests after the rains to graze on the lush grasses of the plains, the Ila would pray to the spirit of the first chief of the Flats, Shandalu, and hundreds of the young men would set fire to the grass and wait with their long spears for the herds of buffalo to appear from the smoke. It was dangerous work, and most years there were deaths and injuries from wounded and angry animals.

One reason for the buffalo drives was to keep them away from the Ila cattle, many of which perished from sleeping sickness spread by the tsetse fly which the buffalo brought with them to the Flats. For the Ila loved and

"Ndi Mwila" – I am a Mwila: Chief
Mukobela, proud in his chiefly regalia,
immortalised in bronze.

valued their cattle above all other possessions, and would neither ride nor work them, and would buy them for their beauty – for a fine voice or unusual horns – and would decorate them with necklaces or bells, name them after a wife or friend. Indeed, the very word Ila comes from "Kuwila", to bring the cattle down from the high ground to the Flats.

The greatest respect that the Ila could pay to the dead was by "Masunto," funeral oxen, the largest animals, slaughtered in numbers according to the importance of the dead: at the death of an important chief, it might be as many as 300 head. About 40 years ago, the Veterinary Department became increasingly concerned at what it regarded as a serious waste of a valuable resource, and Chief Mukobela was asked if it would not be better for him to set a good example and say that only 30 cattle should be killed at his funeral and the value of the rest devoted to a memorial – a school or an orphanage. Chief Mukobela was delighted at the idea, but had two conditions. First, he wanted to see the school at Namwala before he died, and second, he wanted a statue of himself outside it. Government agreed, and Mukobela remains the only Zambian chief to have been commemorated by a bronze statue.

47

LAUNCHING THE "GOOD NEWS"

*A*t Kituta Bay near present-day Mpulungu there is a small stone monument with a plaque bearing the words: "The LMS 'Good News' was built here 1884." Nearby are the derelict remains of a ship. *The Good News*, or *Habari Ngeme*, belonged to the London Missionary Society which, after a survey of Lake Tanganyika in 1879–80, decided that along its shores was "a rich and varied field for Christian missionary enterprise" which could best be served by ship. A Liverpool marine architect designed a two-masted yacht with an auxiliary steam engine 17,4m long and 4m at its widest. When it was completed, it was dismantled into parts small enough – with a few exceptions – for porters to carry as head-loads along African footpaths and deliver them to the African Lakes

The "Good News" in dry dock at Ujiji.

117

Corporation, founded in 1878 in response to Livingstone's call for Christianity and "legitimate commerce" to be brought to the interior.

Every part of the *Good News*, from teak deck to heavy keel and sheet steel, down to the smallest rivet, had to be carried from the coast near Quelimane by river and land and lake to the north end of Lake Nyasa. From here, the last 320km to Kituta Bay were mostly unkown country. The delivery of so large a vessel over so great a distance took the labours of nearly 1 000 porters over 16 months, and was probably the biggest inland expedition Africa had ever seen. Wrote Fred Moir, one of the Scots brothers who founded the ALC: "To induce eight men, untrained to carry loads, to combine to carry the heavy stern-piece, was the crowning problem of each stage of the journey …"

A young engineer, James Roxburgh, was sent out to assemble the ship. It took him sixteen months, and he died of dysentery and exhaustion on 18 May 1885, two months after the *Good News* finally went down the slipway and into the lake. Another sixteen months passed before another engineer was sent by the LMS and she got up steam for the first time under her captain, a former naval officer, Edward Hore. For the next twenty years, the *Good News* plied the lake on missionary work and became a common sight to the dwellers along the shore. Then it was found that tsetse fly had moved into the coastal area, and the people moved away from the danger of sleeping sickness. The *Good News*, no longer needed, was beached and abandoned at Kituta. During the First World War, the Germans shelled her to make sure she was not used against them, but by then she was already beyond repair.

It was nearly 60 years after her launching that the memorial was built of stones from the deserted slipway. The original plaque, bearing the names of the ship's builders, was lost when the memorial was damaged by elephants.

48

THE OLDEST CHURCH IN ZAMBIA

The London Missionary Society was founded in 1795 as a non-denominational organisation to spread the Christian faith beyond Europe; its primary support came from the Congregational Church, and its most famous representative was David Livingstone. In 1880 Edward Hore, Master Mariner of the Society, was looking for a site at the southern end of Lake Tanganyika on which to assemble the *Good News*, the first steel steamboat on the Lake. Hore found Niamkolo "in every way a desirable locality", but "the disturbed condition of the country makes it unsuitable at that time for our purpose." So a site at Kituta Bay, on the estuary of the Lofu, was chosen for building the boat. Niamkolo was established as a mission station during the boat-building period 1883–5, but was then abandoned until 1887, when the LMS returned, reopened Niamkolo and established a second mission, Kawimbe, on the plateau above the Lake.

In May 1893, James Swann of the LMS purchased the Niamkolo estate from the Government of the British South Africa Company, and, supplied with goods which came overland from Zanzibar to Ujiji and thence by the Good News down the Lake, the mission flourished. On 29 August 1895, the cornerstone of a church was laid and the building completed the following year. It was built – and probably designed by – Adam Purves, an industrial helper and teacher at the mission. The church consisted of a main hall of about 10m by 25m and a three-story tower about 5m square and 16m tall. The walls, nearly a metre in thickness, were built of an inner and outer skin of locally-quarried and roughly-dressed sandstone, bonded with mud and anthill. The cavity betwen the inner and outer walls was filled with rubble. Finally, the church and tower were thatched with grass. A visitor in 1965 described how it stands near the cliffside overlooking a bay; behind it are woods, in front of it, long green grass. "It was one of the most beautiful and impressive views I have ever seen ..."

The first church in Zambia was probably built at Feira in the 18th century, but totally destroyed by the time Livingstone passed by in 1856; the church at Niamkolo, completed in 1896, though roofless, still stands as a landmark for craft approaching Mpulungu.

By 1908, however, the Niamkolo area was suffering a high incidence of sleeping sickness, and the staff moved into the hills. Soon afterwards, the mission buildings and the church were badly damaged by fire. For the next half century, the ruins stood deserted: the upper part of the tower crumbled and fell, ants raised mounds on the stone-flagged floor, now open to the sky, and trees rooted themselves in the crumbling walls. The church was built by inexperienced masons, and the bonding was of poor quality; much of it was leached out by decades of rain seasons, many vertical joints opened, and the pressure of the rubble core began to spread the walls. By 1954, it was clear that prompt action was needed if the church was to be preserved, and the LMS handed it over to the National Monuments Commission, which declared it a National Monument in April 1955 and carried out extensive preservation work in 1962.

Adam Purves, the architect and builder of Niamkolo, died at Mbereshi Mission in the Kawambwa district in 1901, and is buried there. His monument is the tower of Niamkolo Church, still a landmark for ships and canoes approaching Mpulungu.

49

THE OLD SLAVE TREE

*I*n the first decades of the 19th century, as the Industrial Revolution spread through Western Europe and the United States, their populations, growing richer and more numerous, created a growing demand for luxuries made of ivory – knife handles and combs, billiard balls and piano keys. By 1870, Africa was supplying 85 per cent of the world's consumption of ivory. Africa's other export was manpower. The European slave trade had ended, but in the clove plantations of Zanzibar and Pemba, in the slave markets of Turkey, Persia and Arabia, it still flourished. In Mozambique and Angola, and in the unknown interior between them, despite official disapproval, it continued. And Europe still bought sugar, coffee, cotton, cocoa and cloves – many of them still grown by slave labour. The search for slaves and elephant pushed further into the interior, and the price was paid in guns and gunpowder … It was Livingstone's highest aim to end the slave trade; and among the slaves he freed from their forked wooden yokes was Chuma, who stayed with him to the end.

Only a minute's walk from the busy centre of Ndola stands a relic of a century ago when slave traders met with slave raiders to talk business. It is a memorial left by nature – a very old mupapa (*Afzelia quanzensis*, or lucky bean) tree entwined by two parasitic fig trees which have almost strangled and obscured it. In the early 1950s, it was suggested that the tree should be protected as a National Monument, and as part of the proof of its history, a statement recorded at Ndola Boma in July 1939 was produced. It was made by an old Arab called Mwalabu, who said he had left Zanzibar when he was about 14. Since he said he had met Dr. Livingstone, who died in 1873, he must have been about 82.

"I know the mupapa tree in Moffat Avenue," he said. "It was in the stockade made by Chimpembeni, Chiwala, Malilo, Saidi Chiwala, Chimbalanga and myself, where we established ourselves after having fought the Belgians. We used to make raids from this stockade, and when we returned, we and the slaves we had captured sat under it. The slaves were not sold and then marched to the coast, but were kept to fight for us or were redeemed by their brethren …"

In 1954, the tree was declared a National Monument, and on 1 April 1957, when Ndola was celebrating 25 years as a municipality, a plaque was unveiled, saying that "this plate has been placed on this mupapa tree to commemorate the passing of days when, under its shade, the last of the Swahili traders who warred upon and enslaved the people of the surrounding country used to celebrate their victories and share out their spoils."

50

REMEMBERING DAG HAMMARSKJOLD

On 18 September 1961, searchers amid the trees 11km north-west of Ndola found the body of the Secretary-General of the United Nations, Dag Hammarskjold, near the burnt-out wreckage of his aircraft. The clearing in which he was found has been made into a memorial to his life and works and a place of pilgrimage for those who remember and treasure his contribution to world peace. A cairn was built of stones brought by young people from all over the world; the Swedish Government presented a huge bust of Hammarskjold. Every year a memorial service is held at the crash site.

Dag Hammarskjold was born on 29 July 1905. He was the son of Hjalmar Hammarskjold, Prime Minister of Sweden. He studied law and economics and taught political economy at Stockholm University. In 1936, he joined the Swedish civil service as under-secretary in the Ministry of Finance, and later became president of the board of the Bank of Sweden. In 1947 he moved to the Ministry of Foreign Affairs and in 1951 was appointed vice-chairman of the Swedish delegation to the United Nations. In 1953, following the resignation of the Norwegian Trygve Lie, he began a five-year term as the UN's second Secretary-General. He began a second term in September 1957.

At midnight on 30 June 1960, the Belgian Congo became the Democratic Republic of the Congo. On 11 July, Moise Tshombe, head of the provincial government of the mining province of Katanga, made a unilateral declaration of independence. The UN Security Council authorised international intervention, and within days the first troops – 4 000 of them from five African nations – arrived in Kinshasa. After a tumultuous year in which the first prime minister, Patrice Lumumba, was murdered, the UN and the Congo Government agreed that Katanga's illegal independence must be ended by force. Bitter fighting broke out between Katangan and UN forces, and a cease-fire was imperative. On

12 September 1961, Hammarskjold left New York for Leopoldville, the Congo capital. UN troops surrounded Tshombe's house, but he slipped through the cordon and got a message to the British consul in Elisabethville saying he wanted to meet Dr. Conor Cruise O'Brien, the controversial UN representative in Katanga, at the Northern Rhodesian mining township of Bancroft.

Hammarskjold, the one man with the prestige, intelligence and understanding to bring a solution to the chaos of Katanga, answered the message himself: he rather than O'Brien would meet Tshombe, and at Ndola, with its full-scale airport, rather than Bancroft: but first there must be a cease-fire on both sides. Tshombe flew in to Ndola and was brought from the Federal Government guest house at Kitwe to wait in the airport manager's office for Hammarkskjold to arrive. The Secretary-General left Kinshasa at 15:51 hours GMT on 17 September in the UN Force Commander's chartered Swedish DC-6B. The flight was made amid tight security and total radio silence until it called Salisbury at 20:02 GMT. The aircraft took a lengthy route to avoid flying over Congo territory, and it was not until 22:10 that its final message was received: "Lights in sight, overhead Ndola, descending ..." Those on the ground, at ten minutes after midnight local time, heard an aircraft flying lower than normal, and heading west of the airport. After that, nothing.

At 22:13 GMT, according to the watches carried by the dead, SE-BDY crashed. The burnt-out remains of the aircraft were not found until 13:10 hours the following day. All 16 aboard were dead except for Sgt. Harry Julian, a member of Hammarskjold's bodyguard: he died a few days later of third degree burns, shock and exposure without regaining consciousness. The body of Hammarskjold himself, thrown clear of the flames, was found curiously composed, half-sitting against an anthill, his body almost unmarked. A few days later, two charcoal burners were arrested after trying to sell a coding machine and two typewriters stolen from the wreckage ... Had they reported the scene of the crash instead of looting it, perhaps Sgt. Julian would have survived, and more would be known of the cause of the crash. As it is, nothing will be known for certain, leaving room for wild speculation. Was it sabotage by the Soviet Union, keen to unseat Hammarskjold as Secretary-General? Was SE-BDY shot down by a Katangese jet fighter? The most likely cause was less dramatic – a bad misjudgement of his altitude by the aircraft's captain, Per Hallonquist, as he made his approach run. He was not familiar with Ndola and had no navigator.

Hammarskjold's death came at a moment when his skill as the world's greatest practical peacemaker were sorely needed to retrieve the

UN position in Katanga. As it was, the fighting continued, and it was not until 15 January 1963 that the Katanga secession ended. The American journalist Smith Hempstone, now a diplomat, wrote at the time: "The story of Katanga is a doleful tale bristling with false morality and injustice ..." And Moise Tshombe? After a period as prime minister of the Congo Republic, he was living in Spain when he was kidnapped and taken to Algiers, where he died in 1969 of a heart attack while under house arrest. He was just 50 years old.

51

CHITUKUTUKU

A century ago, the world's railways were powered by steam, and on the highways huge "road locomotives" hauled heavy goods in trailers. On the farms, steam engines which could provide both haulage and static power drew the plough and powered the thresher. Petrol and diesel engines drove steam power into history just as it was reaching its greatest efficiency, but for a while, steam was king of road and rail and staunch supplier of power to all kinds of industry.

Chitukutuku, the most famous steam traction engine in Zambia, pictured here in retirement at Shiwa Ng'andu in the 1930s, its firebox burnt out after labouring for fifteen years as a source of power and generator of steam.

In the early days of Northern Rhodesia, the first wheeled transport was the wagon, drawn at walking pace by a span of 18 oxen. Doel Zeederberg, the pioneer transporter, speeded up the 165km journey between Livingstone and Kalomo by using relays of trotting oxen. But further up country lay the lair of the tsetse fly and death for the oxen from trypanosomiasis. The steam traction engine, impervious to tsetse flies, came into its own for a while. The first and probably the most remarkable feat of steam traction in Northern Rhodesia began in 1907, when a rough track was cut from Broken Hill, where the railway then ended, to bring equipment for the country's first modern mine at Kansanshi, 500km away. The journey was considerably longer, for the traction engines, pulling trains of trailers, had to keep close to their water supplies and away from rivers they could not cross. The engines were voracious consumers of wood as well as water, and gangs of labourers cut firewood, keeping pace with the steam engines, which moved at much the same pace as the ox-wagon.

Equipment for the development of the Star of the Congo mine in the Belgian Congo was hauled by steam traction engines, and as the railway from Benguela advanced to Beya and then sent a branch line to Kipushi, Kansanshi came within 100km of the line of rail. It is surprising to recall now that the regular weekly service, using two traction engines to carry copper from Kansanshi to the Zairean railhead at Kipushi, ended only in 1929. Traction engines were also used during the early years of the now forgotten copper mines in the Mumbwa district to haul their output to the railway line. The remains of such engines can be found to this day in remote bush areas, but probably no more than two have survived reasonably intact. One of them, a Burrell, was bought during the First World War by John Thom, later famous as a trader and as Ndola's first mayor in 1932–4. It was used at first for stumping farmland, later to power a sawmill, and from 1922 to 1929 it stood in a yard in Ndola and ran a grain mill. When John Thom retired, he gave the engine to the municipality of Ndola, and until 1979, when it went to the Copperbelt Museum, it stood in the children's play park in Blantyre Avenue.

But the most famous of Zambia's traction engines is the 19-tonne Fowler Compound Road Locomotive, No. 13053, which was ordered from Leeds about 1908 to haul the equipment for and operate the machinery of the small factory built on the Chambeshi River, where the Great North Road crosses it, to extract and treat wild rubber collected from bush vines. Until rubber from the vast Asian plantations began to reach the markets about 1910, the tyres of the growing motor industry depended on wild sources, and for a while, even the tiny amounts gathered

127

from vines in the Northern Province promised to be highly profitable to the struggling British South Africa Company's government.

The Fowler and three trailers were unloaded from railway trucks at Kashitu, a few miles north of Kapiri Mposhi, towards the end of 1913, and began the journey to the Chambeshi, over the roughly-cleared track which was to become the Great North Road. It took over 18 months for the engine and trailers to reach the factory on the river bank – and before long it was closed by the demands of the First World War: the rubber gatherers became porters for the army, which needed 150 tonnes of supplies a month, and the factory closed in 1916.

After the war, the Fowler was used to power a saw-bench for building new Government offices in the Northern Province, but by 1922, the engine had long been standing idle, and Government gratefully sold it to Sir Stewart Gore-Browne, who used it to provide steam and power for distilling the essential oils from citrus fruit at his Shiwa Ng'andu estate for 15 years. At its golden jubilee in 1958, it was repainted and set up as a National Monument. It bears the name of all the traction engines. For as they huffed and puffed along their rough tracks in the stillness of the bush of long ago, the people who heard and saw them gave the great machines a name which nicely conveys the sound they made – "Chitukutuku."

52

THE CENOTAPH

The Cenotaph in Lusaka stands directly in front of the Secretariat building, and commemorates the dead of the two World Wars in which Zambians fought and died. It was unveiled on 7 November 1955, 20 years after the capital had moved from Livingstone, by the then Governor of Northern Rhodesia, Sir Arthur Benson, and dedicated by the Bishop, the Rt. Rev. Oliver Greene-Wilkinson.

The Cenotaph, a word taken from the Greek for "empty tomb", was designed by a Government architect, Peter Lawson. He modelled it closely on the original in Whitehall, London, which was designed by the eminent architect Sir Edwin Lutyens, and built in 1919. It omits any religious symbols because of the diversity of those who fought in the war. Like the London original, the Lusaka Cenotaph is exactly 33 feet (9,9m) tall, but it differs in having sword windows on each side which can be illuminated as a visible symbol of remembrance at night. It is built of reinforced concrete faced with local blue limestone. The "sarcophagus" at the top and the steps at the bottom are of the same stone, but saw-cut instead of hewn to give a variation of colour and texture.

The first regular armed forces to serve in Northern Rhodesia were some 120 volunteers from the Indian Army who formed a police force for the British Central Africa Protectorate (Nyasaland) and Northern Zambesia (later North-Eastern Rhodesia) in 1891–3, when they were replaced by 200 Sikhs. Their first operations were to clear off the slave traders; their secondary purpose was to deter the Germans in Tanganyika from expanding southward. When the British South Africa Company took over administration of the north-east from the Imperial Government in 1900, a new armed force was formed, the North-Eastern Rhodesia Constabulary. In South-Western Rhodesia, the first local force was the Barotse Native Police, formed with the help of Paramount Chief Lewanika in 1899. In 1911, North-Eastern and North-Western Rhodesia were amalgamated into Northern Rhodesia, and the two police forces merged into the Northern Rhodesia Police the following year. It was still a military

The Cenotaph bearing the old coat of arms, the Union Jack flying outside the Secretariat: a picture from its early days.

force with only a small section for civil police work.

In September 1914, a small contingent of police fought off a German attack on Abercorn, and there were casualties in skirmishes along the shores of Lake Tanganyika and among a short-lived unit of white volunteers, the Northern Rhodesia Rifles. By May 1916, there were five companies of the Northern Rhodesia Police fighting in German East Africa, and by the war's end had helped to capture a vast area of the country as well as to join the final exhausting pursuit of the German General Von Lettow Vorbeck through Mozambique and Nyasaland and finally to his surrender at the Chambeshi River. Their war memorial is at Livingstone.

The military and civil branches of the Northern Rhodesia Police were separated in 1933, and the Northern Rhodesia Regiment was formed. In the Second World War, the Regiment was expanded to no fewer than eight battalions – five of them front line units which served in East Africa, Somaliland, Madagascar, the Middle East and Burma with distinction. Five soldiers won the Distinguished Conduct Medal, and five the Military Medal.

The Cenotaph now reminds us not only of the sacrifices of many brave men from the 1890s and the defeat of the slavers, through two World Wars, but on to 1964 and beyond, to those of the Zambia Regiment and the Zambia Air Force who have died in the service of their country in war and peace.

53

Nine Dead Soldiers

*I*n the Commonwealth War Graves section of Kansenshi Cemetery, Ndola, may be found the graves of nine South African soldiers who were killed in the crash of a Dakota aircraft on a farm outside Broken Hill on 28 September 1945. Until the death of Dag Hammarskjold and his 15 companions on 17 September 1961, almost exactly 16 years later, it was the worst air disaster the country has ever witnessed. It was a double tragedy in that they were killed not by enemy action, but after the war had ended and while they were happily on their way home.

For months, the South African Air Force had maintained a shuttle service between Cairo and Pretoria to bring home thousands of service-men, most of whom had fought with the Sixth South African Armoured Division in Italy.

By modern standards the shuttle aircraft were small and slow, and the airlift had months more to go before the last of the soldiers were back to the occupations of peace. The Broken Hill crash was not the first fatal accident on the shuttle service: it was the fourth and last. The first was at Kisumu on Lake Victoria when two returning ex-prisoners of war were killed and 24 injured on 11 May. Exactly two months later, on 11 July, all 28 on board were killed when a Dakota crashed into the lake at night. Only six days later, 16 men were killed in a Ventura which crash-landed at Khartoum. News of these disasters was discouraged from spreading among the thousands still awaiting repatriation, but rumours abounded,

A few of the thousands of Rhodesian and South African troops who waited at Cairo West airport for the Dakota shuttle service back home. Some of them never made it.

and some of the troops, though longing for home, cautiously took the option of returning by sea to Durban.

The events leading to the Broken Hill tragedy began to unfold at the Cairo West military aerodrome on 24 September when routine inspection found a small amount of metal deposited in the oil filter of the port engine. After maintenance and a flight test, the aircraft was passed as serviceable, but the flight engineer was told to keep an eye on the oil filter during the southbound journey. The aircraft took off on 26 September with 24 returning soldiers and a crew of four. At Wadi Seidna, five and a half hours' flying time from Cairo, the flight engineer found about half a teaspoonful of metal deposit in the filter, but he was inexperienced on Dakotas, and discarded it as insignificant. Next morning, the aircraft flew on south. It was refuelled at Nchanga and took off at 14:10 on 28 September for Bulawayo.

After about 40 minutes, the port engine began to vibrate and lost power. The gradual loss of height which followed made the captain decide to land at Broken Hill rather than attempt to reach Lusaka. But by the time he neared the railway line to Broken Hill, he realised he could not make the airport and radioed to say he would make a wheels-up landing. He chose a ploughed field near Nyama siding, about 50km by road from Broken Hill. The aircraft slid on its belly and turned 180 degrees. The propellers broke off, one pierced the port fuel tank, and fire broke out.

The crew escaped from the pilot's top hatch, uninjured except for the wireless operator who broke his leg. Fifteen passengers escaped from the starboard emergency hatch, but nine at the tail end, crowded by the main doors, were suffocated and burnt to death. With the exception of the faulty port engine, the port wing and the tail plane, the aircraft was almost completely destroyed. A farmer's wife, Mrs. Bekker, heard the failing engine, saw the aircraft turn and disappear. A cloud of black smoke arose. Before collecting all her bedsheets for bandages and hastening to the crash site with her husband, she sent a servant to alert the home of a railway ganger, W.G. Bremner, who telephoned Broken Hill. Meanwhile, the RAF radio operator at Broken Hill also sounded the alarm, the mine hospital was alerted and a junior Government medical officer, Dr. Cyril Davies, hurried to the crash site. Bremner stopped a passing goods train and the surviving soldiers, after first aid from the Bekkers, had limped to the line and been placed in the guard's van. All but four of them had burnt hands and faces, and the wireless operator's leg was badly broken. They were met at Broken Hill station by St John Ambulance volunteers and taken to the mine hospital's inadequate operating theatre – formerly the mine club's billiard room. Here the railway medical officer, Dr. W.W. Cowen, worked without stopping until 3.30 in the morning dealing with the casualties. From his retirement in England, Dr. Cowen, now 85, recalled the devotion of the two St. John Ambulancemen who volunteered to help in the theatre. "Not being used to this type of occupation, they became physically sick, went outside, brought up, and returned to the theatre to carry on their good work …"

Investigators from South Africa who arrived at the scene less than 24 hours later found that the main doors were only slightly damaged by fire and that there was nothing wrong with them. The inquiry was told that though the passengers had been briefed on emergency procedures, some – excited at the prospect of getting home – were not paying attention, and the instructions did not include operation of the exit handles. The inquiry concluded that the deaths were due to panic and ignorance. Examination of the engine showed that its rear main bearing had collapsed, resulting in crankshaft whip leading to fracture of the rear cam gears. The engine should have been declared unserviceable when metal was found in the oil filter at Cairo West.

The most senior of the survivors was Lt.Col. Harry Klein, a pre-war journalist who had risen through the ranks as a resourceful armoured car commander. In 1994, still living in Johannesburg, he was by then almost certainly the last survivor of the crash. In 1952, he published a book, "Land of the Silver Mist", in which he gave a graphic account of his escape, and extracts from this were quoted in an unsigned article in *The Times* of Zambia of 5 October 1993. It was the first most Zambians had ever heard of the story. Klein's description of his last moments in the blazing aircraft was written from the clear memory of a near-death experience from which, he says, it took him months to recover.

"… A wild panic of fighting, screaming men, in flame and choking fumes. Cold terror when I wrestled with the handle of the rear door, impervious to the licking flames searing the flesh from my hands and arms. The dull hopelessness of despair when the jammed door refused to budge …" Then, he says, someone led him to a small open window: they were the last to escape. The accident report says Klein had "severe burns, hands and face and back of neck."

The bodies were not recovered from the wreckage until the day after the accident. They were first buried in a mass grave in Broken Hill cemetery, in the presence of hundreds of those in the district who were shocked and grieved by the tragedy of young lives cut off just as the days of peace beckoned to them. In November 1971, their remains were removed to the Commonwealth War Graves Commission plots at Kansenshi Cemetery, Ndola.

54

THE CHIRUNDU FOSSIL FOREST

About 20km west of the Chirundu Bridge on the road from Lusaka to Harare, travellers who can spare a few minutes will find one of Zambia's most unusual National Monuments – the petrified remains of what was, 150 million years ago, a vast and flourishing forest. The area of the National Monument is the centre of a much bigger area in which fossilised trees can be found. Tree trunks up to 3m long and 30cm in diameter have been exposed by erosion of the soft red sandstone in which they have lain buried for millions of years.

Archaeologists have found places nearby where Stone Age men lived. These early men used the fossil wood to make weapons and tools not because it was the most suitable but because there was so much of it. The trees have been changed by a process of mineralisation. They were once saturated by water carrying a solution of silica, familiar to most people in the form of sand or quartz, which gradually solidified and, cell by cell, replaced the original cellulose which is the woody constituent of trees. In the end, the fallen trunks became solid masses of silica. In its pure form, silica is colourless, but the presence of a small amount of iron oxide has coloured the logs until they closely resemble the dead timber found lying around in living forests.

The Chirundu fossil trees are described as "conifer-like", and it is some indication of Zambia's changed climate that no conifers are now indigenous in Central or Southern Africa. Pines imported from Asia and America have long been established in Zambian plantations, but they are easily destroyed by fire, and it is unlikely they could grow in unprotected areas.

The Chirundu fossil forest was declared a National Monument in 1954 when it was found that visitors were removing and destroying some of the best specimens.

A log of petrified wood in the Chirundu fossil forest.

LEGENDS AND LORE

55

THE SACRED BURIAL GROVE

Mwalule, in the Chinsali district of the Northern Province, is the traditional and sacred burial grove of the Paramount Chiefs of the Bemba, the Chitimukulu. It is said that Mwalule became the burial grove long ago, in the time of Chiti, son of Mukulumpe, founder of the Bemba people, in the country called Luba. Chiti was killed by a poisoned arrow in a fight with Chief Mwase of the Nsenga. The magician Luchele took the burial party to Mwalule, and there they buried Chiti in an oxhide shroud. The guardian of Mwalule is Shimwalule, who is distinguished from all other royal officials by living to the east of the Chambeshi River. All the others live to the west. Only a very few may enter Mwalule, and no Shimwalule may bury more than one Chitimukulu: if he lives until another dies, he must be replaced.

The Bemba have priest-councillors (Bakabilo) of the Chitimukulu and other senior chiefs, experts on most aspects of chieftainship – ritual, government, the succession of chiefs. The Bakabilo of the Chitimukulu are themselves hereditary holders of titles as old as that of the Chitimukulu himself. The senior Bakabilo of the Chiti are known as the Bashilubemba – six of them, each with important roles in the installation and burial of the Chitimukulu. One of them, Chimba, acts as regent during the lengthy burial rites of the Chitimukulu: the first Chimba was half brother of the first Chitimukulu. Eight Bakabilo, the Bena Tembwe, are the pall bearers who carry the dead Chitimukulu to Mwalule.

There are many stories of the bad luck which follows accidental or deliberate violation of the sacred grove. One of them tells how in 1920, a white district officer was taken to Mwalule by an unauthorised Zambian. A week later, the Zambian was taken from the verandah of his house by a lion. The following year the district officer was killed by a flagstaff at Kasama which fell on him while it was being lowered for painting ...

56
KANAMAKAMPANGA

Seventy-five years ago, three boys from Mukapu's village in Lambaland walked 100km to Kafulafuta Mission in search of schooling. The first was Katontoka, and he wore a loin cloth and carried a rush mat, a puku's skin, a small cooking pot, a spear for protection, and a strong stick. The second was Meleki, who also had his sleeping mat and his buck's skin, an axe and a kalimba with which he made music on the long journey. The third was Kanamakampanga, who had not only a spear, but a bow and half a dozen arrows. When he was born, Kanamakampanga mother's mother gave for his first name the name of his great-grandfather, Chilenga, called Nkombalume, Prince of Hunters.

The small Chilenga soon lived up to his name, setting traps for birds and mice with stones supported on sticks or a noose of home-made string. One day he set a noose on a path marked by the hooves of a buck, and the next day he found he had strangled a reedbuck too big for him to carry, and he became famous when his uncle, Lumetuka, carried it home on his shoulders. From that time, Lumetuka took Chilenga on all his hunts, carrying the bow and arrows while Lumetuka carried spear, axe and muzzle-loading gun. Chilenga learnt the lore of hunting, and when he was about ten years old, his uncle took him to the hunting shrine of the village, with its horns and tails, and put powerful medicine into cuts he made on the boy's right hand, his right arm and his right shoulder blade. Chilenga was now a professional hunter, and to be called Kanamamkampanga.

Each day after school at the mission, Kanamakampanga went hunting field mice to make a relish for the evening meal, or even bigger game, for he was a brave hunter, knowing his uncle had placed two charms, impindo, on his leg. One afternon, he went to visit one of his fish traps at the river. There, in an open space between the trees, a leopard was standing over an antelope it had killed. Kanamakampanga was fearless. Here was meat for the school! He took his spear, moved towards the leopard and shouted at it – "Go away! Go and dress yourself!" – the insulting words used to drive away a dog. This was too much for the leopard. It growled, but turned round and fled into the trees. When Kanamakampanga called on the boys from his school to help him carry the bushbuck, he was truly a hero, and they sung the successful hunter's song:

"Tuya mukondo, tuya – Mbalala"

"Let's go on the trail, let's go, Mbalala!"

57

CHIENGI CHARLIE

On its appearance alone, the lion easily carries off the title of King of the Beasts, and throughout history it has been portrayed as a symbol of courage and fierce independence. In reality, however, the lion is sometimes less admirable. It will eat carrion in preference to the hard work of hunting and killing its own meals, and it will sometimes run away from humans. On the other hand, a single maneater, like Chiengi Charlie, can terrorise a whole district.

The story of Chiengi Charlie belongs to the district of Chiengi on the shores of Lake Mweru in the furthest north of Zambia, and takes us back 85 years to 1909. It is said that Charlie was almost white in colour and had lost half his tail in some battle. Perhaps it was because he was getting old that he found it easier to kill men and women than to catch faster prey. Perhaps it was because he was old that he was so cunning, for he killed 90 people before he was finally killed himself.

Charlie seemed to recognise poisoned meat and seemed to have an uncanny ability to avoid traps. He was known to kill within a hundred metres of a patient watcher with a gun. There seemed to be no end to his terrible exploits. Until one day he met Galatea, the ex-askari who was mail runner for the Boma. Charlie came out of the bush in front of Galatea on to the mail path, and sat before him on his haunches like a great dog. Galatea's wife was with him, and he told her to climb a tree. Then he started to ram five fingers of black powder into his old muzzle-loader. The lion sat motionless. Galatea loaded buckshot down the muzzle of his gun. The lion did not move. Galatea moved slowly forward: the lion crouched, his lips drawing back into a snarl. Galatea fired, and for a moment awaited his fate as the kick of the old gun crunched into his shoulder, and the noise and smoke of the gunpowder cleared.

Then he turned about. "Woman," he shouted. "Come down from the tree and pick up the bag." Chiengi Charlie, half his skull blown away, lay dead at his feet.

58

AN AERIAL ADVENTURE

*I*n a corner of the Anglican Cathedral of the Holy Cross in Lusaka may still be found a disused eagle lectern. It has been repaired after accidental breakage, but the simple beauty of the carving and the incised inscription in its Hoptonwood stone still mark it as the unmistakeable work – probably the only example in Africa – of the English sculptor and typographer Eric Gill. The inscription is from Psalm 139: "If I take the wings of the morning … Even there shall thy hand lead me …" It commemorates the dramatic events of the week which began on the last day of February 1935. At that time, private aviation was a daring hobby carried out in single-engined, open cockpit aircraft by pilots who were rarely women. One of its devotees, however, was Margaret, Lady Young, wife of the Governor of Northern Rhodesia, Major Sir Hubert Young. She possessed her own aircraft, VP-NYA.

On 28 February 1935, she took off from Livingstone at 8:10 in the morning with a senior Government medical officer, Dr. T.R. Kerby, for a three-hour flight to join her husband in Lusaka, which was then about to become the new capital. Unnoticed, her compass worked loose from its mounting, and the frail aircraft drifted off course until it returned to the Zambesi, where to their horror they realised they were over the Kariba Gorge and not the Kafue. Without a map of Southern Rhodesia, and with fuel running low, Lady Young looked for a landing place. She chose what appeared to be a lightly-covered mealie patch near a village. The maize turned out to be very tall millet which entwined itself round the undercarriage as they landed and pulled the aircraft slowly over. Lady Young bloodied her nose, but otherwise they suffered only bruising, though the aircraft was badly damaged.

In Lusaka, Sir Hubert waited in vain for his wife to arrive. At 12:15, an hour after their scheduled time of arrival, he called for an intensive search. Two aircraft already at Livingstone took off, and soon there were 12 – including five from the South African Air Force – all of them sweeping over the wrong area between Livingstone and Broken Hill. Sir Hubert

143

commandeered a special train and moved fretfully up and down the line. On the ground, troops, police and Government officials meticulously searched the wrong places. Sir Hubert's ordeal, prolonged for nearly four days, might have been longer but for the intervention of good luck and modern technology.

The village near the crash site was Mushami, near the Kariba Gorge, and the excited villagers happily escorted them back there where they learnt that by chance a storekeeper, G.W. Cameron, temporarily engaged as a locust ranger (the 1930–45 plague was then at its height) was camped not far away. He fed them, gave up his tent to his distinguished guest, and sent a runner to the nearest Government station at Gokwe, 150km away. The messenger reached Gokwe on Monday 4 March. By good fortune, the district commissioner was the enthusiastic possessor of an amateur radio transmitter and he soon called up a fellow "ham" in Bulawayo. The story was by now world news: for the Bulawayo Chronicle it was the greatest of all Rhodesian aircraft stories and it was reported at length which today would only be matched by coverage of a major catastrophe.

Meanwhile, Cameron and the grounded aviators set out on 2 March for civilisation. Lady Young, footsore after a first day's march of 20-odd km, transferred to a rough machila she designed herself. They travelled slowly for five days, but made their rendezvous with a senior police officer with car at Sweswe on Thursday 7 March, just a week after the crash. Lady Young finally joined her husband after a flight in the pride of the fleet of the Rhodesia & Nyasaland Airways, a Westland Wessex, carrying champagne, aspirin, quinine and the Southern Rhodesian Minister of Defence. In Lusaka, the Governor invited all the searchers to a sundowner party, and doubtless it was at these celebrations that someone first coined the joke for which the episode was remembered by many when nearly all other details had faded: that Lady Young had preserved her virtue from any designs which Dr. Kerby might have had upon it by carrying a bag of apples. For Sir Hubert, his wife's safe return to him and their three young sons was a matter for sober and sincere thanks and appropriate commemoration. He commissioned the lectern for the then parish church of Lusaka. It was a long time before Gill completed it, and it was finally blessed by Padre Hobson and used for the first time in the presence of Sir Hubert's successor, Sir John Maybin, on 1 September 1940.

59

BEER

*B*eer, says the encyclopaedia, "is the generic name for alcoholic beverages made by fermentation of extracts derived from cereal grains or other starchy materials." Beer was known to the ancient Egyptians, and it is doubtless from there that the art of brewing seeped down the length of Africa. In Zambia, traditional beer is usually made from the small grains of sorghum or millet, or from maize. Methods differ from place to place, and strength varies according to the degree of fermentation. Four or five days is about the usual time for good beer. Here, in detail, is a recipe for a strong beer which takes far longer to mature. It begins with grain put in a calabash with water for three days. Then the water is poured off and the grain left for another two days while it sprouts. A second batch of grain is then soaked, dried the next day, and ground into a fine flour, boiled and set to cool. The malted grain of the first batch is now crushed and added, well worked up with the hands, and left all next day. On the following day, the mixture is cooked. Next day it stands, and on the following day, the mixture is cooked. Next day it stands, and on the following day more malted grain is added. Meanwhile, more grain is stamped and soaked in water and the next day crushed and boiled and then added to the mixture. Then more meal is cooked and mixed up and added. Next day, the beer is ready for drinking. This recipe takes not much less than two weeks, and reflects the seriousness with which the brewing of beer is taken.

For Zambians, the making and drinking of beer is an essential part of traditional life, far more important than the part played by wine or beer in Europe. It plays an essential part in the economy of food production: laborious operations are carried out by collective parties of kinsmen and neighbours to whom beer is offered as incentive or reward. It plays a part in communal rejoicings, accompanied by music and dancing – at a wedding feast, or at the initiation of young people – or it may be offered to the spirits of the dead. It is not only a drink, but a food on which it is possible to live exclusively. It is, in consequence, an important attribute in a wife that she is able to brew good beer.

It is brewed most commonly in the harvest months from May to August, depending on the size of the crop: in a poor season there may be beer only at a chief's court.

Where honey is readily available, as in the North-Western Province, another kind of beer can be brewed from it. Honeycombs filled with young bees are mixed with honey and water and set near a fire or in the sunshine to ferment. Honey beer is ready for drinking within 24 hours and is highly intoxicating. Because of the speed with which it is made, and its strength, honey beer became popular in the early days of the Copperbelt, when the mines asserted a legal monopoly of brewing for their beerhalls – where the beer had a maximum strength of 4% and was often weaker. Where honey was not available, sugar or treacle could be used. From South Africa, where thousands of Zambians used to work in the gold mines, came skokiaan, a potent drink made principally from sugar and yeast, but often containing a variety of other substances. "It is made quickly, in one day ... On this night it has mealie meal, sugar, tobacco, methylated spirits, boot polish and yeast ..." For Zambians living near the borders of Angola or Mozambique, a knowledge of distilling from grain, mashed bananas or sweet potatoes became widespread, and a strong spirit called kachasu (from the Portuguese cachaca, rum) can be found.

A hunter of a century ago described meeting a happy chief with "eight wives and his legion of daughters who produce for him such abundant harvests that he has materials for making beer from January to December. When he is satiated with this beverage, he can fuddle himself with palm-wine which they make from the borassus, hyphaene and phoenix palms, so common in the district ..." (The sap of *Hyphaene ventricosa*, the vegetable ivory palm, can be drunk as palm wine or distilled to produce a spirit; the flower-spikes of *Borassus aethiopum*, the borassus palm, can be tapped for palm wine; and palm wine can be brewed from the fermented sap of *Phoenix reclinata*, the wild date palm.)

In modern times, and especially in the towns, where half the population now lives, the opaque African grain beer has been largely displaced by the industrial-scale manufacture of a clear beer made from barley and flavoured with hops. But traditional African beer has also been industrialised, distributed in tankers or sold in packets. These packets need to be shaken to put the sediment into suspension, and such is their popularity they gave their name to a Lusaka street – "Sheki-Sheki."

60

MWANAMBINYI'S HOLE

Among the many fables told by the Lozi people is the story of Mwanambinyi's Hole. Those who recite the tales of the royal tradition relate how, four centuries ago, the chieftainess Mbuyamwambwa pre-empted a coup d'detat against her by appointing her son Mboo as the first Lozi king, and herself as the power behind the throne. But Mboo quarrelled with his brother Mwanambinyi, who had become a great warrior, and in a contest between their favourite bulls, Mwanambinyi lost, and led a magical exodus of his people and their cattle to the south of the flood plain.

Until about half a century ago there was at Imatongo, not far from Senanga, a small hole in the ground. It was said that this was all that remained of the enormous pit made by Mwanambinyi at the foot of the sand belt and into which he led all his soldiers and most of his cattle. They were never seen again, and Imatongo is known as Mwanambinyi's sitino, or royal grave. At times, it is said, people living near the sitino, hear cattle lowing, cocks crowing, women pounding grain. Sometimes it is said the war drums of Mwanambinyi can be heard, and on a still night, his spirit drums as well. At one time, a caretaker was appointed to live near the hole in case the great warrior ever decided to return, and he said he often saw Mwanambinyi's hunting dogs in the night. The nalwange, or white egret, may be seen in hundreds near the sitino, and these are said to be Mwanambinyi's cattle, for the hole was not big enough for all of them, and he had to change the remainder into birds.

Imatongo became a place of tribute, and travellers journeying south on the Zambesi always stopped at Mwanambinyi's sitino to leave an offering to ensure a safe passage through the rapids. About 1900, when the rains were late, and the crops were dying, King Lewanika made a pilgrimage to Mwanambinyi's Hole. He carried a pot of water from the river and placed it at the Hole to show what was required. A white missionary who was present scoffed at the ceremony. But the next day it rained. It is said that when the same missionary refused to let his paddlers stop at

Mwanambinyi's Hole, and preached to them on idolatry, the biggest and most heavily laden of his boats was turned over and he lost all his goods … Only forty years ago, it was known in Sesheke that two white men who scorned the ceremony found that no matter how hard they ran the engine of their boat, it would not move until tribute had been paid … Mwanambinyi's Hole disappeared half a century ago, but the place was marked with a mwinda, the sweet-smelling violet tree which has many medicinal and magical uses.

61

THE LEGEND OF THE KONGAMATO

The Kaonde people of the North-Western Province used to carry charms called "muchi wa Kongamato" to protect them at certain river crossings from the Kongamato, "the overwhelmer of boats." This fearsome creature had the reputation of living downstream, where it exercised its power of stopping rivers in their flow, causing a sudden flood which could overwhelm a boat. The creature was described by the Kaonde of old as a huge red lizard with membranous wings like a bat spreading five or more feet, and with teeth in its huge beak. No-one saw the Kongamato and lived to tell the tale; and since it was immortal, no remains of it were ever found. It could not be killed by any missile – it simply swallowed them.

In the 1920s, Headman Kanyinga from the Jiwundu Swamp area near the Zairean border instantly identified as Kongamato a picture of a pterodactyl, the extinct flying reptile with a slender teethed bill whose fossils in East Africa are estimated to be over 136 million years old. But headman Kanyinga had no scale to compare the drawing with Kongamato: the pterodactyls were quite small, some no bigger than sparrows. Nevertheless, as recently as 1958, the science journalist Maurice Burton wrote in the *Illustrated London News* in 1958 that there had been several reports from Africa of a pterodactyl-like creature, with speculation that the Bangweulu Swamps might be one of its habitats. He pointed out that off the coast of Africa, the coelacanth, a deep sea contemporary of the pterodactyl, had been caught by fishermen …

But the excitement was short-lived. Experienced ornithologists in Zambia identified the likely source of the pterodactyl stories: the whale-headed or shoebill stork *Balaeniceps rex*, a bird a metre or more tall, of bizarre appearance. But it does not altogether explain away the Kongamato. For though the shoebill stork with its huge beak has been seen around Bangweulu, in Mweru Marsh and even (in 1943) in the Itawa Swamp near Ndola, it has never been seen in the Jiwundu Swamp.

62

THE HARE, THE ELEPHANT AND THE HIPPOPOTAMUS

A Bemba fable tells how the hare was taking a walk one day, carrying a long rope. He met an elephant. "Let us have a tug-of-war," said he, "to see which of us is the stronger." "You are trying to fool me, Hare," said the elephant. "You are no bigger than one of my back teeth. I'll pull you with my trunk and toss you into the sky." "Maybe, maybe not," answered the hare. "Just let me put this rope round your neck. Then I'll go down to the river, and I bet you won't be able to pull me back here." The elephant agreed to humour the hare, and let him put a loop of rope around his neck. The hare uncoiled the rope as he walked back to the river, where he found a fine big hippopotamus. "Let us have a bet," said the hare, "I'll tie this rope to you and go up the hill and you won't be able to pull me back to the river." "Hare," said the hippopotamus, "I can throw a canoe in the air with one toss of my head. Are you stronger than I am?" "I don't know," said the hare. "Can I tie this rope to you so that we can find out?"

So the hare tied the rope to the hippo, ran half way up the hill and hid in the bush. The two huge animals began to pull against each other, and they pulled and pulled until they both grew tired and walked towards each other. "What!" shouted the elephant. "It's you, Hippo, that I have been pulling! "I thought it was the hare," they both said together. "Let's find him and kill him!"

They found the hare close by, tied him up and hung him from the branch of a tree. While they were gathering firewood to grill him, a hyena came by. "Hello," he said." "What are you doing there Master Hare?" "Alas," sobbed the hare, "the hippo and the elephant have tied me up because they want to make me eat bones, and my teeth aren't right for cracking bones." "Oh ho," laughed the hyena. "I am the one for that. I will take your place!" And with one snap of his powerful jaws he cut the rope and set the hare free. When the elephant and the hippo returned with the

151

firewood, they were surprised to find the hyena in the hare's place. "What are you doing here?" they asked simultaneously. "The hare told me that you wanted to make him eat bones, and he can't, so I have taken his place. Now, where are these bones?" "Here they are," said the elephant and the hippo. And they threw their loads of firewood on the hyena which flattened him out and killed him. Then they set fire to the wood and burned him up.

Kashimi kapela. (The tale is told.)

63

CHISOLO, THE GREAT AFRICAN GAME

Over much of Africa, in villages and towns – in the shadow of a tree, in the shade of a building – you are sure to find a small piece of dusty ground with rows of shallow holes arranged in four lines, perhaps with small stones in some of them. In towns after work, in villages after the harvest, you will find two players squatted facing each other, putting stones in or snatching them out of the holes – playing with such bewildering speed that the onlooker has little idea of what is going on.

They are playing a game which has many names – nsoro and chisolo are two names common in Zambia – and with many variations in the number of holes and with rules that differ according to where it is played. Usually the four lines consist of ten, twelve or fourteen holes, but sometimes more. It is not unlike the game of draughts. The motive of the game is, by moving the stones in certain directions fixed by the rules, to get them into positions relative to your opponent and to "eat" or "snatch" his "men" from the board. The true skill lies in choosing the move which will bring your men into a winning position. Generally a game will consist of only 20 or so moves, but according to the skill of the players – and the number of holes and stones – it may take a hundred or move moves to complete.

BUILDERS AND BUILDINGS

64

LUNDAZI CASTLE

One day in 1948, a tired district commissioner sat under a mopani tree in the Eastern Province and thought about building a Norman castle. The site for the castle was Lundazi, and the man who made this odd dream come true was Errol Button, who retired after Independence as permanent secretary to the Ministry of Lands and Natural Resources – a title well suited to his character.

Button's changes to the face of the little station of Lundazi began with a water shortage. There was a swamp where the Lundazi and Msuzi rivers met, but according to the engineers of the Department of Water Development and Irrigation, it was an unsuitable site for a dam. Button decided to ignore professional advice and went ahead anyway. There were no bulldozers at Lundazi – not even a spare wheelbarrow. So grass baskets were used instead to carry soil to build the dam wall. The dam filled up, the engineers predicted disaster – and Button raised the dam wall until there was a lake of some 20 hectares. It was not for forty years that the professional engineers were proved right: the dam burst in 1990.

But this was far off half a century ago, when tourism was coming to life, the number of visitors to the Luangwa Valley and the Nyika Plateau was increasing, and a night stop was needed. Button was allowed a budget of £500 – about £8 500 in today's terms – to build a Government rest-house. It was not a very large sum of money even for the austere and simple bungalow doubtless envisaged by the Secretariat in Lusaka. But sitting under the mopani tree after chasing a rogue elephant around the Valley, Button decided that the most attractive, if not the most appropriate building to occupy the splendid site he had chosen overlooking the dam, would be a small castle in the style of those built in England after the Norman invasion of 1066. He made a rough sketch there and then on the back of a cigarette box – the universal notebook of those days – and took it back to the boma where he transferred it in more detail to paper, and called in the boma builders.

Years later, Button recalled that the work went ahead with amazing speed because the builders could not wait to see what it would look like when it was finished. When the final brick was laid, the head bricklayer turned to his friends. "When I grow old," he said, "I will show my grandsons this, and they will turn to each other and say: 'Such an old fool could not have built this!'"

The fruit of their labours was a single-storied castle with double-storied towers at each corner, and half a dozen bedrooms for tired travellers. It lacked only a name, and this was provided by Button's little daughter, who called it "Rumpelstiltskin" after a character in a German folk tale she had been reading, and the name is recorded on a plaque set in the wall. The castle became so popular with tourists (who approved, among other things, of bream from the lake caught just before breakfast) that one side was extended in 1952 to double the number of bedrooms – bringing the cost of one of Zambia's most interesting buildings, and its most unusual hotel, to a bargain price of £2 000, or about £29 000 in today's money.

Norman battlements looking over the Zambian bush. Errol Button had a budget of £500 to build it.

65

THE CATHEDRAL OF THE
HOLY CROSS

When the capital moved from Livingstone to Lusaka in 1935, the town planners placed a cathedral site about midway between the Secretariat and State House, but it was never built there. It was not until 1952 that the Diocesan Synod of the Anglican Church resolved to build one. On 2 August 1953, a great cross of Zambian teak was dedicated on the present site, and for long it stood as a reproachful reminder that the youngest city in the Commonwealth had no cathedral.

Progress, hindered by lack of money for such a building, was slow at first. The campaign was given thrust and direction in typical fashion by the then Archbishop of Canterbury, Dr. Geoffrey Fisher, when he preached at the cathedral site and launched the appeal for funds on 17 April 1955. "I exhort and encourage you to make haste to build your Cathedral … Go to it. Do it all without a break, giving glory to God. And may it through the centuries be a grand possession and inspiration to the Church in this Diocese …" By October, the fund had reached £40 000, and in 1956, a local architect, Dick Hope, joined later by Ian Reeler, was given charge of the project. On 11 July 1957, the foundation stone was laid by Queen Elizabeth the Queen Mother.

The central principle of design laid down by the Diocese was that "the building should be shaped by worship, and not worship by architecture." A cathedral of "traditional" design could not be afforded, nor would it have been appropriate to a young country in Africa. The funds available for the building, a modest £100 000 – about £1,2 million today – meant that the planned spire, transept windows and main porch screen had to be omitted, and that it had to be simple in design and materials, using reinforced concrete, partly clad with local stone on the exterior, some white painted roughcast plaster for the interior. Much depended on the skill of the builder in setting concrete at great heights and at awkward angles, said Dick Hope: Harold Mitchell, the contractor and a former mayor of

There are some visual echoes of Basil Spence's 1951 design for rebuilding Coventry Cathedral in Hope and Reeler's 1956 conception for Lusaka's Cathedral of the Holy Cross.

the city, was a master carpenter and "he worked with heart and soul."

The windows are framed in precast concrete carrying coloured panels of Perspex graded from dark and sombre at the back of the nave to the brightness near the sanctuary. The interior was designed to be used as occasion demands: all parts may be used separately or together – important in a cathedral to be used mainly as a parish church. The high altar is the focus, placed on the crossing of the two axes of the scheme; it stands beneath a baldachin (canopy) from the top of which rises a gilded steel cross recalling the dedication of the building.

On entering the west door, one is immediately faced by the font, which symbolises the spiritual rebirth of man; while the central position of the lectern and pulpit bear witness to the teaching mission of the Church. The choir does not occupy its traditional position between the altar and the congregation, but is at the west end above the entrance, where, together with the organ, it can best lead the congregation in song.

The Cathedral of the Holy Cross was opened for use in 1962, and the altars consecrated at the opening service. In 1963, the roof was covered, appropriately for Zambia and because of its permanency, with copper sheeting. It was formally consecrated in 1970 when it was at last fully paid for.

66

THE VICTORIA FALLS BRIDGE

"*I* want to get there at once," Cecil Rhodes said in 1897. "There is little satisfaction in knowing the railway will reach there after one's death …" He was speaking of the Victoria Falls, and his ambition remained unfulfilled. When the railway reached the Falls on 25 April 1904, he had been dead for two years and one month. But his dream of a railway running from the Cape to Cairo was still alive, and for its most dramatic river crossing, the Zambesi, he had a special plan.

The cheapest and simplest solution would have been a bridge at Kandahar Island, 10km up-river, but Rhodes ordered a bridge slightly downstream, across the great gorge of the Zambesi. "I should like the spray from the Falls to dash against the railway carriages", he said, and when the wind is right, it does so. The first survey of the site was made in 1900–01, and Rhodes lived long enough to approve it and the preliminary design of the bold and handsome steel arch bridge which claimed to be the highest in the world. It is about 117m above low water in the gorge, 930m above sea level. George Pauling, the contractor who built the railway, hoped to build the bridge too, but his tender was much above that of the Cleveland Bridgebuilding and Engineering Company of Darlington in England. "I was sorry we had not the honour of building the bridge, but honour of that kind can be purchased at too heavy a price," he wrote in his autobiography. Cleveland's price was £72 000 – about £4,25m at today's prices – for a bridge 212m long and weighing 1 644 tonnes. (This weight slightly increased in 1930 when the decking was rebuilt to accommodate a 4m roadway.)

When Pauling's sister triumphantly drove the first locomotive to reach the Zambesi in 1904, preparations for bridging the Victoria Falls had already begun. The first crossing of the gorge in 1903 was achieved by a light line carried by a rocket. This was then tied to a heavier line, and that to a steel rope which could carry a bosun's chair or a 2m square wooden box on sheave wheels, drawn by a windlass on each bank. The first man to cross it was Charles Beresford Fox, nephew of the bridge's designer, Sir Douglas Fox. He was followed by a few hardy workers and even a few foolhardy tourists at 10s a time. It took about ten hair-raising minutes. Later that year, Fox, who had come to work on the foundations of the bridge, nearly became its first casualty. He and Percy Clark, the pioneer photographer and curio dealer at the Falls, decided to become the first to reach the bottom of the gorge from the south side. Fox, according to Clark "a reckless sort of Johnny", attempted too much and got stuck, then fell 30m from a wet rescue rope into a tree from which he was, unconscious and in considerable danger, brought to safety. His rescuer, Jack Whitton, died a pauper in Ndola 40 years later, his only possession the engraved clock he was given for his bravery. To the credit of the contractors, there were only two fatal accidents during the entire construction period.

For the final construction of the bridge, a separate, much heavier cable was laid upstream from the bridge site. This had an electric winch which could handle loads up to 15 tonnes. Electric cranes handled the huge steel sections on either side of the river as they were extended across the gorge, and the actual erection took only nine weeks. So accurate were the calculations that when the centre was reached and the last piece of bottom boom ready to be lowered into position, it was only necessary to wait for the cool air of 6 o'clock in the morning for the booms and bracing to meet exactly – and on 1 April 1905, they met, exactly a year from the start.

The official opening, which took place on 12 September 1905, was conducted by Professor George Darwin, son of Charles Darwin, past president of the Royal Astronomical Society, president of the British Association for the Advancement of Science, and then in the year of his knighthood. It is said that an elderly member of his distinguished party, wishing to calculate the depth of the gorge, picked up a pebble and took out his watch to time its fall. Absent-mindedly, he dropped his watch into the gorge and timed it with the pebble.

67

TAZARA, THE FREEDOM RAILWAY

*C*ecil Rhodes had a vision in 1889 of a railway line running uninterrupted from Cape Town to Cairo. At that time, 75 years of world-wide railway development were coming to an end, though none could foresee what the internal combustion engine was about to do: petrol engines, diesel engines and jet engines were soon to drive railways into recession. But in 1889, Rhodes could draw inspiration from the tremendous railway ventures in the United States and Canada to foresee a railway running up the continent of Africa as a similar artery of development. His vision was never realised, and never will be. But at the end of the First World War, when Britain took over Tanganyika as a League of Nations mandated territory in 1919, it raised among enthusiasts the idea of a railway link between the Rhodesias and the East African coast, and a railway magazine excitedly predicted Tabora as "the Clapham Junction of Africa." At that time, trade between East Africa and the Rhodesias was negligible, and seriously discouraged by the rough track with the grandiose title of "The Great North Road." The development of the Copperbelt in the 1920s had no effect other than to suggest a greater movement of dried fish southwards to feed its growing population. The copper, lead and zinc went south or west by rail.

With the outbreak of the Second World War, the Great North Road was used as it had been in the First War, as a military highway to serve the troops in the north – in Ethiopia and in Somaliland this time. At the end of the war in 1945, with an idealistic Labour government in power in Britain, development schemes for Africa were discussed and planned: the most expensive of them the vast failure of the groundnut scheme in Tanganyika in the late 1940s. Undeterred, a new generation of colonial planners began talking of a railway link between the southern highlands of Tanganyika and the Northern Province of Northern Rhodesia to bring its farming potential to reality. Paid for by the British and United States

Governments, a six-man team from the distinguished engineering consultants, Sir Alexander Gibb & Partners, set out to report on the possibilities. Their final report, published in 1952, concluded the rail link could not be justified and that the region would be better served by a network of roads. The traffic forecast for a railway was depressingly low, accepting there would be no change in the export routes from the Copperbelt.

It was not until the end of Federation in 1963 and the impending independence of Tanganyika and Northern Rhodesia that the subject of a railway connection between them was raised again. Julius Nyerere, first president of Tanzania, and Kenneth Kaunda, first president of Zambia were both enthusiasts for it as an engine of development for remote areas of their countries. In September 1962, UNIP published its manifesto for an election to be held under a new constitution leading to the independence of Zambia. It included a map showing a proposed railway link with Tanzania, which had achieved independence in the previous year. "Tiny" Rowland, engaged in building Lonrho into an Africa-wide empire, lost no time in offering to finance another survey – a rush job, mostly carried out by helicopter – which was presented in November 1963. It papered over some of the cracks in the argument, and was severely damaged by a World Bank survey, also requested by Kenneth Kaunda, which bluntly rejected the railway in favour of a far cheaper road. A 1964 UN report on the development of the Zambian economy by the economist Dudley Seers, was equally condemnatory.

But there are times when politics take priority over economics. In February 1965, President Nyerere of Tanzania went to China on an official tour. Chou En-lai, the Chinese premier, was knowledgeable and sympathetic … in May, a team of Chinese surveyors was on its way, and in June the Chinese made a firm offer to build the line. The Western nations kept quiet, only paying for a further survey from London consultants who predicted up to five years to build, using the latest construction methods, and a total cost of £138 million. It failed to impress Western governments. Then, on 11 November 1965, Ian Smith made his unilateral declaration of independence. Zambia was effectively cut off from its export routes, for the Benguela railway through Angola had negligible spare capacity. Emergency routes had to be opened at speed, and the Great North Road became the "Hell Run," while an airlift brought in emergency supplies of fuel. An Italian company was given a contract to build an oil products pipeline from Dar es Salaam to Ndola. On 6 September 1967, China, Zambia and Tanzania agreed on terms for an interest-free loan to build the railway for £167 million.

The building of the railway, China's greatest aid project, and one of the greatest engineering feats of the last half century, began with the arrival of Pu Ke, leader of the Chinese work team, at Dar es Salaam on 26 July 1969. He was the first of an eventual team of 25 000 Chinese and 50 000 African workers. At the base camp of Mang'ula, 300 men worked three shifts a day, six days a week, making 2 000 sleepers a day. At Zingari, 800 men produced 8 800 cubic metres of rock a month. From China came 310 000 tonnes of rails, 330 000 tonnes of cement. Construction camps were built about every 60km, keeping ahead of the work, then dismantled and reassembled further down the route. At Mpika, the biggest of the base camps, a permanent engineering workshop took shape ...

Some of the Tanzanian terrain was daunting: in the Mlimba-Makambako section of 170km, by the Great Ruaha River in Tanzania, where the land rises nearly 1 300m in 1 000km, there are 47 bridges and 18 tunnels. The pillars of the bridge over the Mpanga River are over 50m high. Nevertheless, by unrelenting hard labour – and helped by the far easier terrain in Zambia – laying the 1 860km of track between Kapiri Mposhi and Dar es Salaam was completed in the first half of 1975, and trial operations began in October. Tazara is designed to carry 2,5m tonnes in each direction each year, and to carry passengers along its length in 40 hours. There are six main and 141 local stations. The tenth anniversary of the official opening of Tazara was celebrated at the New Kapiri Mposhi terminus on 16 August 1986 in the presence of President Kaunda of Zambia, President Ali Hassan Mwinya of Tanzania, and Mme Chen Muhua, State Counsellor of the People's Republic of China. In the decade they were celebrating, Tazara had suffered landslides, floods, accidents, equipment shortages and failures – and even the destruction of bridges by the Rhodesian rebels in 1979. Now the enemy is economics. The cost of the railway has not yet been repaid, and the reopening of trade with South Africa, peace in Mozambique and falling Zambian copper production have hit traffic hard. Now the railway is facing a new battle to commercialise itself, to make a new contribution to the development and success of the countries it serves.

68

CAIRO ROAD

It would be hard to think of a more famous street in Southern Africa than Cairo Road. According to Lusaka's first historian, Richard Sampson, the name was first suggested about 1923 by a local farmer, Albert Dunbar, in a conversation he had with the district commissioner, Gibson Hall, at the corner of what is now called Chiparamba Street. Until that time, none of the six streets which comprised Lusaka had a name, and the main road running north and south through the village was just called "the front street." Dunbar's suggestion was taken seriously, and in November 1924, the six streets, led by Cairo Road, were officially christened.

The origins of Dunbar's little joke lie in the history of the internal combustion engine. By the outbreak of the First World War in 1914, the motor car was beginning to achieve respectable standards of reliability, but long distance driving was still something of a hazard. To drive from Cape Town to Cairo – or from Cairo to the Cape – was considered a great adventure and a true test of both vehicles and drivers who had to negotiate very long stretches without anything deserving the name of road. Lusaka lay inescapably on this route, and its citizens saw many such expeditions in the years between the wars. One of the first and best recorded of them was that led by a British army officer, Capt. R.N. Kelsey, in 1913. The cost of it was paid by the now long-dead Argyll Motor Co. of Glasgow as an advertisement for its products and by the London newspaper, the Daily Telegraph, which sent a journalist to report on the expedition. It came to a dramatic end not far from Chitambo Mission. Kelsey, an inexperienced hunter, wounded a leopard and committed the fatal error of pursuing it into thick bush. Despite the courage of his African companion, who pulled the leopard off him by its tail so that Kelsey could shoot it, he was badly mauled. By the time he had been carried to the reclusive Dr. Storrs – who had long since given up practice to hide himself on land he bought from Chirupula Stephenson at Chiwefwe – Kelsey was dying of gangrene. The Argyll was sold to the Rhodesia Katanga Junction Railways, and it was used for several years on the completion of the Benguela railway. The proceeds of the sale went to pay the wages of a member of the expedition, Euain Wilson. He came back to Ndola after the First World War as Colonel Wilson, became its mayor in 1940, and served as Member for Health and Local Government in the Legislative Council from 1948 to 1954.

The first local car to travel down Cairo Road was Percy Morton's in 1917. At that time, the "front street", as it was still called, was a deeply rutted track suited only to oxwagons, and he soon transferred to the railway reserve between the road and the railway line to journey to and from his house a kilometre or two to the south of the village. After the First World War, there grew sufficient owners of private vehicles to form a Lusaka Automobile Club whose main aim was to pressure the impoverished government of the BSA Company into improving the roads and, when it failed, to undertake much of the work themselves. The village was built on limestone and was flooded in almost every rain season, when the foot-deep dust turned to mud and huge pools of water lingered for months. In February 1926 unusually heavy rains led to such appalling conditions that the medical officer of health seriously suggested the township should be evacuated. Instead, a deep drainage ditch was dug from one end of Cairo Road to the other, a landmark for 30 years. It was also a public hazard for unsuspecting travellers who, leaving the railway station in the darkness, could easily fall into it as they hastened towards the welcoming lights of the Grand Hotel, and there was more than one drunk who drowned in it.

By 1952, Cairo Road was still lop-sided, with commercial development lining the west side of the road, and virtually nothing on the east side except the railway station. The railways said it would cost £400 000 to move the line to the west so that the old town and the new could join up; the money was not forthcoming – and eventually road over rail bridges replaced the level crossings at what was probably even greater cost. But eventually a town plan was agreed, and in 1955–6, amid scenes of engineering turmoil and mountains of limestone, the east side carriageway was completed and in the following two years, the whole commercial area was remodelled. The Cairo Road canal was lined with stone and covered with concrete slabs and turfed; flowerbeds flourished on the corners. There was even talk of renaming the remodelled road, but that was quickly silenced. Cairo Road retains its romantic name.

69

THE HOUSE AT CROCODILE LAKE

*I*n January 1914, when the Anglo-Belgian Boundary Commission completed three years' work defining the borders between Northern Rhodesia and the Belgian Congo, one of its members, a young British army officer, left Ndola for the north. His name was Stewart Gore-Browne, he was 31, and he was in search of a farm to come to when he left the army. He had thought of the Hook of the Kafue, but the Bemba he had met on the Commission's work persuaded him of the beauty of their country. "One day – it was April 10 – we suddenly came upon what I thought was the most beautiful little lake I had ever seen … I knew at once I had found what I was looking for …" It was Shiwa Ng'andu, the Lake of the Royal Crocodile, whose exact location is 11.12S, 31.45E. It is 650km from the railhead at Ndola – in those days a three-week journey on foot and by canoe via Kapalala, Lake Bangweulu and the Chambeshi River.

Within hours of his arrival, Gore-Browne had killed his first rhinoceros and earned his Bemba name – Chipembere, the animal with the fearsome temper: it was well chosen, for only in old age was his tendency to alarming eruptions of anger mellowed. He began at once to prepare his farm, felling trees for timber, buying fruit trees from the White Fathers' mission at Chilonga. But the war came in August 1914, and it was not until 1920 that he returned, a well-decorated lieutenant-colonel, to his little lake in the remote Northern Province, 100km from the end of the nearest road at Mpika.

The governing British South Africa Company was offering free farms to ex-soldiers, and Gore-Browne persuaded three others to join him in an imaginative scheme to extract the essential oils of roses, peppermint and geranium – crops of sufficient concentration and value to stand the costs of the journey to the markets of Europe. He added 10 000 acres at a shilling an acre to his grant of 3 000 acres. Already he had formed in his mind the shape of the great house he would build.

There were many difficulties in the early years. His partners left, and Gore-Browne worked on, learning by hard labour and hard experience. In 1927 he went to England to bring back his bride, Lorna Goldman, and by 1931, he was ready to crown his efforts by building the house he had dreamed of for her and their daughters. He made a model and drew the plans of a building of startling grandeur. It was to have a great hallway, a courtyard of guest rooms; a house with its own chapel and library. With Joe Savill, a soldier he had known in the war, with Mulemfwe, the head capitao, with 128 bricklayers and a million bricks, the house was completed in 1933 – except for the imposing tower he added to the front in 1938. It had cost about £5 000 in materials (about £165 000 in present-day values), and there was nothing like it in the whole country, certainly not Government House in Livingstone, a conversion of a modest hotel

Nothing like it in the whole country: Shiwa Ng'andu, designed by a monocled former artillery officer, built with a million locally-burnt bricks; despite its remoteness, "the guests – governors, other dignitaries, wandering missionaries and the like – arrived in increasing number to sample the cuisine, culture and boundless hospitality of Shiwa Ng'andu..."

referred to by one of its inhabitants as "the abattoir" and by another as "an unbecoming bungalow."

The estate prospered, at first from the export of the essential oils of the bitter orange, of limes and geranium, eucalyptus and lemon grass; the community at Shiwa Ng'andu grew. It had its own schools, hospital, shops, post office and aerodrome. Then a virus disease destroyed the lime orchards, and the value of the essential oils from oranges was drastically cut by competition from a cheap synthetic, the estate had to exist on timber, butter and beef – and on Gore-Browne's private income.

Despite the isolation of his estate in the far north-east of the country, Gore-Browne's name and reputation grew with his increasing interest in the politics of Northern Rhodesia; the visitors' book at Shiwa filled with the names of almost every important visitor to the territory. In 1935, he was asked to stand for the Northern electoral district of the Legislative Council. It led to a long period in which he tirelessly represented the interests of the African people. In 1945, he was knighted for his services to the country. He retired from politics in 1951 – though he gave early support to Kenneth Kaunda's UNIP, and his biographer wrote truly that "without him, Zambia would have emerged with poorer endowments and more racial bitterness." He died, aged 84, on 4 August 1967. The year before, President Kaunda had made him the first and only Grand Officer of the Companion Order of Freedom. But he also treasured the words of Elias Mtepuka, editor of the *African Weekly*: "You've a black heart under a white skin." Sir Stewart Gore-Browne was buried, in the presence of President Kaunda, in a grave on a hill overlooking the lake he had first seen 53 years before, where he had written that he wanted to make "a life work of the black people."

70

THE SAUCEPAN RADIO

*B*roadcasting in Northern Rhodesia began in 1941 with a small short-wave radio station. It was operated from a single room at Lusaka's little airport building, draped with blankets to reduce aircraft noise. It was supposed to keep people informed of the progress of the war, to stimulate the war effort, and to convey instructions if there was an emergency. Broadcasting hours were short, reception was unreliable, and anyway, few people had receiving sets. District commissioners, missionaries and the mining companies saw to it that clusters of loudspeakers were nailed to poles or hung from trees in the townships; on the evenings when the brief broadcasts went out, traders and farmers brought their radios outside, volume turned up at full blast to attract listeners. The programmes were written and broadcast by Northern Rhodesia's first information officer, Kenneth Bradley, appointed to the job by the Colonial Office in 1939. When Bradley was transferred to the Falkland Islands in 1942, the resident magistrate at Broken Hill, Harry Franklin, was appointed to succeed him and to found an Information Department. Franklin was a man of unusually liberal opinions for those days, based on a wide knowledge of African ways. Radio, he predicted, had a great future all over Africa, a continent in which speaking and listening were the basis of intellectual life – the source of customary teaching, of folklore, riddles, plays, argument – and music.

At the end of the war, Franklin proposed a fully-fledged radio station broadcasting exclusively to Africans. With British Government aid, it was developed as the Central African Broadcasting Station, serving, in seven languages, the then Southern Rhodesia and Nyasaland as well. The shortage of listeners was at first tackled by extending the provision of community receivers at mission stations, chiefs' courts and bomas. Though where these were heard, the "wayaleshi" was a magical success, there would be no mass audience without cheap receivers. For three years, Franklin wrote round the world to find a company which would make a cheap, tough, portable, dry-battery short-wave receiver. Those available at the time cost £45 – the modern equivalent of about £700: such cost-cutting inventions as the transistor were still a decade away.

When Franklin went on leave in 1948, he told his staff that unless the problem could be solved, he could not justify continuing the broadcasting service. In Britain, he travelled round the radio manufacturers in

A carefully-posed photograph by the Government photographer, Nigel Watt, of a suitably happy family listening to a Saucepan Radio in 1950.

search of his ideal portable: none were interested. At last he remembered a friend from Broken Hill who had married the chairman of the Ever Ready battery manufacturing company, Magnus Goodfellow: perhaps he would be interested in selling radios at cost, making his profit from the batteries. He was, and with a senior BBC engineer, Bill Varley, Franklin was soon invited to see two prototypes – one round, one square. "I chose the round one," Franklin recalled years later. "If was accidentally dropped it would roll and not smash a corner." It was made of aluminium alloy. "Just like a saucepan without a handle," said Varley. "That's what it is," said Goodfellow, "there's a saucepan factory up the road. The square one is a biscuit tin. We'll make a dozen samples of the round one. What shall we call it?" "The Saucepan Radio," said Varley – and the joke stuck. An Ever Ready marketing man came to Lusaka to test the market: £5 for the radio, £1 5s for the big external dry battery, about the size of a brick, which lasted about 300 hours. Most were sold on the spot, but the marketing man was not yet convinced. Franklin took an unauthorised plunge. "Government will buy 1 500 sets," he said … It was enough.

Helped by generous-minded distributors in Northern Rhodesia, the blue-tinted Saucepans were sold at minimum profit, making them probably the cheapest in the world, while the engineering section of CABS provided an exchange system for breakdowns – usually the fragile glass valves. By 1950, bomas, libraries, welfare halls and a growing number of private homes had the new "Saucepan Radios" with eager audiences …" For ages I have been feeling lonely," wrote one of many enthusiastic listeners. "Now I have the whole world in my house." Other Commonwealth countries heard of the Saucepan, and the Queen of Tonga bought a hundred of them for her people. Broadcasting transmissions improved geatly in the succeeding years, and the transistor revolutionised receivers. But the arrival of television in Kitwe in 1961 and in Lusaka in 1964 drew off much of the time, talent and money from radio so that Zambia has still not achieved the network of regional broadcasting stations which would put good quality listening – and locally-made programmes – within reach of all.

Harry Franklin, under the terms of his first appointment to the Colonial service as inspector of schools in 1928, was entitled to retire at the age of 45, and in 1951 he did so, with an OBE. He held the nominated post of Member – Minister – for Education & Social Services in the Legislative Council from 1954 to 1959, and after election for the Central Africa Party in 1959, was Minister of Transport & Works in 1961–2. He farmed near Lusaka, became a journalist and author, and at last retired to England, where he died in 1995, a few months short of his 90th birthday.

71

THE LIVINGSTONE MUSEUM

*I*n 1930, the sum of £100 was included in the budget "for the purchase of ethnological objects for a Museum." It was the inspiration of a pioneer administrator, J. Moffat Thomson, who had come to the country with the African Lakes Corporation in 1901, and had become at length Secretary for Native Affairs. The Governor, Sir James Maxwell, a firm supporter of the project, told all district officers to look out for suitable articles and to buy them. The resulting collection was housed in a store room next to Thomson's office. In 1934, Maxwell's successor, Sir Hubert Young, even more of an enthusiast, found the collection its first home – the old magistrate's court in Livingstone – and in 1937 established the Rhodes-Livingstone Institute "to be engaged upon anthropological research, and upon the work of studying the many problems that arise when black and white peoples come into constant contact." Its work and publications achieved international recognition, and it is now the Institute for African Studies of the University of Zambia.

In 1934, the only memorial in the country was the monument at Chitambo's to David Livingstone, and Young had the idea of establishing the museum as a memorial to Livingstone, and of siting it by his most famous discovery, the Victoria Falls. Its first title was "The David Livingstone Memorial Museum," and its first handbook, printed in 1936, listed 405 exhibits including bark cloth, decorated lechwe skins, woven cotton cloth, beadwork, metalwork, woodwork, mats and baskets, musical instruments and divining apparatus. It had seven letters from Dr. Livingstone (one presented by Sir Hubert Young, the others by the South African mining magnate Abe Bailey), 29 ancient maps of Africa – and a replica of the skull of Broken Hill Man – *Homo rhodesiensis*. The museum's first permanent home was the old United Services Club, to which it moved in 1937. It was an improvement over the magistrate's court, but the collections still suffered from theft, clumsy handling and insect damage.

A larger and more elaborate handbook published in 1937 showed a total of 842 exhibits, and in the following year, the first professional curator was appointed: Desmond Clark, fresh from first class honours in archaeology at Cambridge, whose 23 years at the museum were to make it world famous and to win him an international reputation and a professorship in California. Driven by Clark's skill and enthusiasm, a building fund was opened in 1945 and the present building was opened as the Rhodes-Livingstone Museum – it reverted to "Livingstone" alone in 1966 – by the president of the British South Africa Company, Col. Sir Ellis Robins, in 1951. It was designed in the Spanish-American style favoured by W.J. Roberts, a government architect from Southern Rhodesia, and built round a hollow square. The clock in the 20m tall tower was given by Harry and Eli Susman, pioneering farmers and ranchers, to mark the 50th anniversary of their arrival in Livingstone.

The staff was tiny. Mrs. Clark was museum secretary, there were two unskilled part-time women assistants – and Ranford Sililo, a gifted artist and model-maker. "One had only to ask for something – bees for a hive in the hunting case, a head on which to display lip plugs or ear ornaments, or a canary for the Chokwe bird case – and he supplied it quickly and efficiently," Clark recalled years later. Under his direction, the museum's collections were expanded, new projects undertaken, and the galleries organised to tell the story of mankind in Zambia, beginning with the tools and weapons of prehistoric man, the beginnings of Bantu penetration, passing on to Bantu technologies and tribal groups. In the historical gallery, Arab and Portuguese, Livingstone, Rhodes, the early missionaries, gave way to modern industry. The museum is still famous for its collection of Livingstone relics and its collections of the material culture of the Central African Bantu.

In the 1960s, the addition of a research wing and a natural history wing greatly expanded the original museum to enable it better to fulfil its original triple role – to collect and preserve material for posterity, to carry out research, and to educate the public. Today, the museum, though short of funds, maintains a collection of over 12 000 specimens of traditional cultural material, 5 000 historical items and 20 000 natural history specimens. It has four specialist departments – history, prehistory, ethnography and art and natural history, four permanent galleries, a temporary exhibition gallery and a craft shop. It is a centre not only of collection, research and education, one of the finest museums in Africa, but also a major tourist attraction with its associated Maramba Cultural Village and Railway Museum.

72

THE GREAT NORTH ROAD

*T*he Great North Road probably took its name from the old road from London to Edinburgh, at a time when imaginations in Africa could still conjure up visions of a broad transcontinental highway stretching from the Cape to Cairo. To Zambians it has long been most closely associated with the stretch of road that runs from Kapiri Mposhi to Tunduma, our lifeline to the sea at Dar es Salaam. Its origins lie in the early years of this century, when the price of raw rubber rose to extraordinary heights as motor vehicles began to infest the roads and large profits were to be made

The Great North Road's finest hour – the Hell Run, when sanctions cut communications with Ian Smith's illegal Rhodesian republic and Zambia, only a year old, fought off economic strangulation with battered, overloaded lorries roaring through the clouds of dust.

even from the laborious collection of tiny amounts from Landolphia vines growing wild in the bush. The cruelties associated with the collection of wild rubber in the Belgian Congo became an international scandal. The British South Africa Company, ever anxious to stimulate the long-awaited return on its investment in Northern Rhodesia, encouraged its one-man Department of Agriculture, the genial Dutchman Josselin de Jong, to regularise and industrialise what had been the province of wanderers trading in little bundles of rubber along with ivory and other odds and ends.

In 1913, after a tour lasting many months, De Jong announced that a factory to extract rubber from Landolphia roots and vines would be established on the Chambeshi River at 10.58S 31.04E – 400km as the crow flies from the line of rail at Kashitu. The machinery for the factory was to be hauled from Kashitu via Chiwefwe, Ika, Chansa and Mpika. For this purpose, a Fowler steam traction engine and three trailers were ordered from Leeds, and a £700 contract for cutting a track 6m wide from Kashitu to Chansa was awarded to Chirupula Stephenson at Chiwefwe. (He surveyed it in the dry season of 1913 with Moffat Thomson, who for ever after claimed they were so short of water they had to drink elephants' urine.) Cutting the rest of the track was to be arranged by the District Commissioner at Mpika.

Construction began with the traction engine chugging close behind the gangs clearing the track. Deviating to avoid steep gradients or to find water, with lengthy delays from breakdowns, bogged down throughout the rains, the traction engine took 18 months to arrive at the Chambeshi on 18 May 1915. The factory did not last long: the war made more urgent demands. It became instead an important staging post on the route to keep the troops supplied in the war in East Africa – hundreds of tonnes a month were needed. The Chambeshi was a crossroads for the Ndola-Kabunda-Lukulu-Kasama route on which carriers, canoes and motor transport were used, and the Kashitu-Kasama road which was extended and upgraded to take motor transport organised by Major Cecil Duly, later a prominent motor trader in both Rhodesias.

By the time the war ended in 1918 – at the Chambeshi crossing – the road to Tunduma was well established, its verges littered with the debris of wrecked and broken wagons and lorries left by years of military transport. But it was a recognisable road, and in 1925, the Northern Rhodesian delegates to Lord Delamere's unofficial East African conference at Rungwe Mission in Tanganyika boldly made the journey from Livingstone and back by car. The first regular motor service between Broken Hill and Abercorn – a five-day journey – began in 1927, and practically all Government passengers and goods for the Northern and Eastern

Provinces travelled by this route. With the outbreak of war in 1939, the Great North Road was soon back in its military role, carrying heavy traffic through to Nairobi for the Ethiopian and Somaliland campaigns. It was so well maintained by the military that one convoy of 300 vehicles passed through with one single loss – a headlamp glass.

By the early 1960s, with good maintenance and better motor vehicles, it was possible to make the dusty journey from Kasama to Lusaka in a long day's driving. But the Great North Road's finest hours followed Rhodesia's unilateral declaration of independence on 11 November 1965 – a bare year after Zambia's own, and legitimate independence. Sanctions agreed with Britain cut Zambia's links with the south, and the Great North Road became the "Hell Run", with Zambia-Tanzania Road Services, formed in 1966, and its sub-contractors hauling at its peak in 1975 a total of 660 000 tonnes – exporting copper, importing virtually everything Zambia needed to survive until the Tazara railway took over the burden in 1976. The toll in lives and vehicles was heavy. In 1966, a £6,5 million loan from the World Bank set in motion the rebuilding of the road to heavy duty tarmac.

73

THE GREAT EAST ROAD

*I*n the earliest colonial days, when Fort Jameson was the capital of North-Eastern Rhodesia, its only commercial link with the outside world was the footpath to Tete on the Zambesi, where steamers plied to Chinde at the river's mouth. Along the footpaths, carriers laboured with 20kg headloads of tobacco, cotton, beeswax, silkworm cocoons, red chillies and ivory. As the economy of the North-East developed, the "Tenga Tenga" system was replaced by ox wagons moving along a rough track to and from Tete, prey to marauding lion, trees brought down by elephants, deep muddy damboes. Next came motor roads, with lorries plying between Fort Jameson and Limbe in Nyasaland, where the railway, built between 1904 and 1919, linked up with the line from Beira to Umtali and the Rhodesia Railways system. The only gap was at the Zambesi ferry, and that was not closed until the opening of a bridge nearly 4km long in 1935.

For the pioneering civil servants, there had been another route from North-West to North-East, on foot or cycle, or carried in a machila – a hammock on poles. For them, the arrival of the railway at Broken Hill in 1906 was a blessing, reducing the walk to Fort Jameson to 500km. With a tent, a cook and about 40 carriers for his goods and stores, the newly-posted civil servant could expect to climb the high wall of the Muchinga Mountains, descend the deep trough of the Luangwa Valley, and arrive with luck at Fort Jameson in not much more than a month. Until 1924, when it was changed to the rail and road route via Beira, the weekly mail was carried from Broken Hill via Mkushi, Serenje and Msoro by red-uniformed runners. They took three weeks to the day to reach Fort Jameson, resting nearby until the Boma bugler prepared for his 3pm call on Thursdays. Then, at the very minute of the hour, they would come jogging proudly in.

When the first Governor of Northern Rhodesia, Sir Herbert Stanley, moved into Government House in Livingstone on 1 April 1924, there was still no more than the mail paths between Broken Hill and Fort Jameson. To visit his Eastern Province, he and his retinue had to travel through

Southern Rhodesia, Mozambique and Nyasaland. Sir Herbert was not pleased by this international itinerary, and in July 1925, a young district officer stationed at Petauke was told to survey and demarcate by visible beacons what appeared to be the most feasible route. The Goverment surveyor who followed him in 1926 moved the route further south and closer to the Mozambique border. With some help from 300 soldiers, a roughly aligned and completed Great East Road was carved out in a couple of years. It was no highway: much of the early traffic was lorryloads of recruits for the Copperbelt, and they took a fortnight – more if the rivers flooded and the primitive pontoons failed, bridges had collapsed or damboes trapped the wheels. It was not until 13 May 1934 that the then Governor, Major Sir Hubert Young, formally opened the 275m Beit Bridge across the last and greatest obstacle on the road, the Luangwa River. After Independence, the Great East Road had its most difficult sections realigned, and the whole length was tarred, so that the journey from Lusaka to what was now Chipata, could be covered comfortably in a day.

74

THE UNIVERSITY OF ZAMBIA

"*L*ess than a thousand young men and women with school certifi-
cate, less than a hundred who have been to university," exclaimed
Kenneth Kaunda. "That was the extent of our supply of educated
Zambian manpower at midnight on 23 October, the moment of our
Independence. Of all the hard accusations we have made against colonialism, that must surely represent a condemnation which it is impossible to
refute." No-one tried to. There were some excuses, but they were as inadequate as the system of education itself. The Rev. Maxwell Robertson, principal of the school at Lubwa Mission, which Kaunda himself attended,
started Northern Rhodesia's first secondary school there in a single hut in
1938. It was probably his example which shamed the colonial government
into opening what was then called the Munali Training Centre in 1940.

In 1933, a year after the opening of Makerere College in Uganda, the
Currie Report gave a solemn warning: "We believe that the passion of the
African for higher education, properly guided, may prove to be a boon to
the economic, social and cultural development of the country, and an
advantage, support and ornament to British rule. Neglected, it must create
social and political confusion." Nothing happened. Another 16 years
passed before a committee reported the the establishment of a college of
higher education in Lusaka was "a matter of urgency." Nothing happened.
Two years later, in 1951, the Carr-Saunders Commission on higher education in Central Africa urged "the immediate foundation" of a university
college in Lusaka. This time progress was frustrated by Federation and the
opening of a university in Salisbury in 1957.

Serious planning for a university in Zambia began with the report of
the Lockwood Committee. It was published in November 1963, just 30
years after the warnings of the Currie report, just a month before the ending of Federation opened the way for Zambia's independence in 1964. Sir
John Lockwood was a former Vice-Chancellor of the University of
London, a distinguished classical scholar and educationist with special
experience of Africa. The deliberations of Lockwood and his colleagues

The hard, grey, long outline of the University of Zambia, cradle of Zambia's thinkers and doers.

emphasised two fundamentals – that the university "must combine practical service to the nation at a critical time in its life, with the fulfilment of the historic purposes of a university as a seat of learning, a treasure house of knowledge and a creative centre of research." Lockwood and his team were also acutely aware that higher education was Zambia's most urgent need. To produce the huge number of educated people the country needed, the first essential was a supply of well-trained school teachers. As a Nigerian academic, Dr S.O. Biobaku, pointed out at the time: "To provide good elementary schools, you need well-trained teachers who have at least good secondary education. Good secondary schools pre-suppose good graduate teachers – and graduates are produced by universities. One hopes they will become teachers and so provide the real pivot of Africa's educational development."

The Lockwood Committee proposed a four-year course following good "O" level passes which would bring students up to an internationally accepted degree standard. The new leaders emerging from the university would educate other Zambians to the same level, creating an expanding torrent of young, trained minds to lead the development of the new nation. The nucleus of the new university consisted of the Institute for

Social Research, the old Rhodes-Livingstone Institute, founded in 1937, and the Oppenheimer College of Social Service which opened in Lusaka 25 years later. The College was able to provide welcome accommodation for the first students.

By the end of 1965, the university's provisional council and the project team were at work on the main campus on the Great East Road, helped by a contribution of £1 million from Britain and half a million from the University Appeal Fund, much of it raised from small contributions, sometimes in the form of peanuts, poultry or dried fish rather than cash, some of it raised by children and by the poor in the remotest villages as well as the city streets and from big business. The architect planner, Anthony Chitty, chose for the material of the new buildings the harsh reinforced concrete of the 1960s "New University Movement" of which the most effective part is the library, an open-plan with 17 decks leading off a central ramp. The landscaping of the 240ha university grounds, which include four lakes now named after Prof. Lameck Goma, the first Zambian vice-chancellor, give Lusaka what has been described as "the city's nearest approach to a public park."

The first 312 students were enrolled in March 1966. President Kaunda, in his opening address, warned them against pride. "It would not promote 'One Zambia, One Nation' if we eliminated tribal differences only to have them replaced by class distinctions so alien to our traditional way of life. Education is a great boon, but it can also be a great curse if it creates an elite of black gentlemen, remote from the masses, conscious only of what society owes them, not of what they owe society. The sacrifices of the people of this country would be in vain, if the University they struggled to found produced graduates whose one thought was self – not service ... The elite we want to foster is one which is more concerned with its responsibilities than with its rights, an elite dedicated to the noble task of nation-building, however hard and humble the demands ..."

The University produced its first graduates in May 1969.

Today the University of Zambia employs a staff of about 2 700 in academic, technical, administrative and other categories to serve a student population of 4 600 in nine schools producing doctors, lawyers, engineers, agriculturists, veterinarians and scientists as well as teachers. Its history has not always been smooth, and its progress has been impeded by Zambia's economic difficulties. But it remains an institution of immense importance to the future of Zambia, touching the country's life at almost every point.

75

THE NATIONAL ASSEMBLY

*T*he gleaming copper which covers the walls of the chamber of the National Assembly on the Great East Road is a splendid introduction to visitors arriving in the capital from the airport. The Assembly building dominates the hill on which it stands just as the hill dominates its surroundings. Indeed, it is said long ago to have been the site of the village of Chief Lusaka after whom the capital is named.

The building of the home for Zambia's Parliament was completed in May 1967, only three years after the site was chosen. The brief for the architects of the Public Works Department was to produce within one month a design whose appearance would state in striking simplicity its power and its purpose – its function as the heart of the nation, the centre of all development. The unusual urgency of the commission – one of such importance that it might ordinarily have been spread over several years – made it necessary to reverse the usual process and to design the dramatic exterior first and to plan the interior afterwards. The choice was made from 80 sketches made in endless overtime, and work began at once on developing the design of a building 73m long by 51m deep on four levels. But despite the urgency of the project, there was time for thoughtful detail such as the symbolic – and anonymous – incorporation into the building's walls of samples of stone or wood from 128 administrative districts of Zambia.

Lusaka designer Mick Pilcher worked with the architects in producing a marriage of modern concrete with traditional African forms – a basic wall mural pattern of the chevrons found in many African arts and crafts, and this is used in several different forms in the Assembly. In the great windowless parliamentary chamber, three of the Zambian colours – orange, red and black – are used in the murals, and the fourth colour – green – in the upholstery of the seats. Everywhere possible, Zambian woods have been used, while for the exterior of the chamber, the choice was inevitable – copper sheeting to shine out in celebration of the source of Zambia's wealth. On the table of the House stands, when the Speaker is in the chair, his staff of office and symbol of parliamentary authority, the mace. The Zambian mace was designed by Zambian artist Gabriel Ellison and made in London. It is 107cm long with an ivory shaft and copper claws holding amethysts at the copper base and head. On copper collars are engraved "Republic of Zambia" and "One Zambia – One Nation."

76

A CAPITAL MOVE

*I*n 1926, a drilling programme proved the existence of vast reserves of copper minerals at the country's centre and promised the beginnings of a great industrial complex. The capital of Northern Rhodesia was Livingstone, on the southernmost border, and although the Governor, Sir Herbert Stanley, was a little doubtful of the Copperbelt's future, he had to admit that a new and more appropriate capital site was "a subject of perpetual agitation and disputes." These were chiefly between those who thought Livingstone not only badly placed but unhealthy as well, and Leopold Moore, pioneer chemist, proprietor of the Livingstone Mail, and the country's leading settler politician, who championed the town's right to remain the capital. Stanley's successor, a rather cantankerous former medical officer, Sir James Maxwell, tended to side with Moore: he liked Livingstone. But the Colonial Secretary, Leopold Amery, ruled from London that immediate consideration should be given to the best site for a capital "having regard to health, communications, and the improvement of contact with the industrial and commercial communities." In the end, the area chosen for investigation lay along the line of rail between Chipongwe, half way between Kafue and Lusaka, and Kashitu, about 75km south of Ndola. A team comprising two doctors and an engineer concluded in March 1930 that anywhere north of Broken Hill was subject to invasion by tsetse fly, and that the healthiest and most convenient area lay between Lusaka and Lilayi, a farm a few kilometres to the south. The Colonial Office called for independent consultants – E.C. Bartlett, of Sir Alexander Binnie, Son & Deacon, a distinguished partnership of consulting engineers, and the Professor of Town Planning at London University, Stanley Adshead. In 1930, the Northern Rhodesian budget had been balanced for the first time, and optimism was in the air.

Lusaka itself owed its origins to S.F. Townsend, Chief Resident Engineer of the Rhodesia Railways in Bulawayo. In planning the route of the railway line 30 years earlier, he marked loop lines at intervals of 30km or so, wherever there was suitably flat ground. Lusaaka's Kraal happened to be 30km from the previous loop at Chipongwe. Lusaka, as it became known, was translated by a knowledgeable official as meaning "a wilderness." It was, and is, the windiest place in Central Africa; Leopold Moore was quick to trumpet from the still, moist air of the Zambesi Valley that the new capital site was "the most arid, desolate, miserable spot in Northern Rhodesia – windswept, cold and miserable." When Adshead disembarked from the train in Lusaka in August 1930, at half past one on a winter morning such as Moore had described, it was very much a frontier outpost, meriting no more than two lines in the official railway guide, and no decent time of arrival. Arising early in the grey daylight, one of Adshead's first observations, as he walked through the dust of Cairo Road, was at the junction of the Great East Road – a notice warning that blackwater fever was prevalent.

But Adshead and Bartlett found Lusaka had an excellent underground water supply, three hotels, two banks and several large stores. Their preliminary survey reduced eight possibilities to three. Chilanga was finally discarded because of an unreliable water supply, and the long low ridge south and east of the Great East Road was preferred, because of its proximity to the railway line, to the ridge at Emmasdale north of the township. A detailed plan followed, and in 1932, a South African architect, Jan Hoogterp, who had had a hand in the building of New Delhi and Pretoria, and was then practising in Nairobi, was flown down to design the main buildings of the new capital. But the timing was unlucky.

In 1931, the Legislative Council approved the spending of £50 000 on preliminary works. But elsewhere in the world, 1931 was a truly awful year, and disaster soon reached Northern Rhodesia. A world conference of copper interests decided that only drastic cuts in production could keep the industry alive. Northern Rhodesia's quota could be filled by only two of the five mines then developing. The others were closed on New Year's Day 1932. There were savage retrenchments in Government and a tax on the salaries of the survivors. The Adshead plan, by now much modified, needed a fairy godmother to save it. On Empire Day, 24 May 1933, Maxwell's successor, Sir Ronald Storrs, was able to say he had found two: the Beit Trust, which guaranteed the interest payments on a loan of £300 000, and the Colonial Development Advisory Committee which made a grant of £130 000 to pay for electricity and water supplies and a restricted building programme.

The restrictions included lopping a wing off the design for Government House, and dispensing with the quadrangular buildings intended for each side of the Secretariat. Cathedral, university and museum alike faded into the future, and there were many other economies so that when Prince George laid the foundation stone of the Secretariat on 4 April 1934, there was still a lot of long grass around what the earlier inhabitants soon nicknamed "Snob's Hill." The official date for Lusaka's attainment of its new status as capital was fixed for the celebrations of King George V's silver jubilee in May 1935. A month or two before, a special train had brought the civil service and its families up from Livingstone. A young district officer with literary ambitions, later to become Sir Kenneth Bradley of the Commonwealth Institute, composed a book "Lusaka: the New Capital of Northern Rhodesia", and a social programme unlike anything the town had ever seen culminated in the ceremonial opening of the Secretariat, the half-built Gymkhana Club and the aerodrome, while the annual agricultural show was moved from Kafue for the occasion and centred on the as yet unoccupied new premises of the Government Printer, the largest covered area in the country. "The whole affair," said the *Bulawayo Chronicle*, "was a brilliant social success and a thoroughly enjoyable entertainment." The week's programme lacked only one advertised event: the military tattoo, cancelled because the Copperbelt was enduring its first strikes, and the troops had been flown in …

SOME CHARACTERS

77

KING LEWANIKA OF BULOZI

*I*n 1823, Sebituane, chief of a Sotho tribe in what is now the Orange Free State, a great leader and fine warrior, led his people north, through the countries of the Tswana and across the swamps and deserts of the Eastern Kalahari. Some time in the 1830s, they crossed the Zambesi at Kazungula, attracted by the cattle herds of the Ila and Tonga people, but also as a defence against attack by Mzilikazi's Ndebele. About 1840, inspired by a prophet, Sebituane turned west to the country of the Lozi on the flood plains of the Zambesi. There they settled, and Sebituane's people married their women to Lozi men, and by this means established the supremacy of their language, Kololo, over Luyana, the ancient language of the Lozi.

But the Kololo came from the healthy highlands of South Africa, and they soon became weakened by the malaria of the Zambesi Valley. When, in 1864, a Lozi aristocrat, Njekwa, advanced on the Kololo, they were massacred, and the Lozi prince Sipopa became king. But he ruled through terror, and in a revolt of 1876, he was killed and succeeded by a young nephew, Mwanawina, who was in turn driven out in 1878 and replaced by a young prince from another branch of the family. His name was Lubosi. Royal rivalry continued and in 1884, Lubosi was expelled from his capital at Lealui. But he rallied his supporters, defeated his enemies, regained the throne, and thereafter called himself "Lewanika", the Conqueror.

King Lewanika of Bulozi, photographed in 1902 in the outfit chosen for him by King Edward VII for the Coronation, the full dress uniform of a British ambassador. "No African ruler of his time achieved more, and none was more regretted..."

Apart from an ultimately unsuccessful coup in 1864–5, King Lewanika ruled

Bulozi from 1878 to 1916. He began by a thorough and merciless purge of his many enemies and by placing close relations in charge of three new provincial councils. He revived and extended the ceremonies of kingship, and developed the ivory trade westwards to Benguela on the Angolan coast and southwards down the Zambesi. He perceived the value of white missionaries, and in 1886 the French Protestant Francois Coillard founded his mission at Sefula.

In 1889, Rhodes obtained the charter for the British South Africa Company which gave him the power to make treaties with African rulers and to exclude his rivals from Portugal, Belgium and Germany. Lewanika's foreign policy was dominated by fear of Lobengula and his Ndebele warriors, and he welcomed British protection, already recommended by his Christian friend, King Khama of the Ngwato. With Coillard's encouragement, but not without misgivings, Lewanika signed treaties with the Company, giving it mineral rights in exchange for promises of protection and development. But the treaties also limited the Company's authority in ways unknown in the rest of its jurisdiction, and which have reverberated down Zambia's history to the present time.

There were long delays in providing the representative of the Queen that Lewanika had asked for, and Robert Coryndon, the first Resident Commissioner, may well have disappointed Lewanika at first: he was only 27, and accompanied by an insignificant handful of unarmed police. He had, however, great charm and ability, and quickly made his mark. Coryndon for his part found in Lewanika a man of great dignity of bearing, a friendly smile, a quick, nervous manner of speaking. He was a good horseman and good with animals, a skilled wood carver, affectionate to his family, inquisitive for knowledge: a man of honour and intelligence.

Lewanika for long cherished a desire to meet Queen Victoria, but the Boer War intervened in 1899, and the Queen died in 1901 before it was over. It was arranged that he should attend the Coronation of King Edward VII, and he sailed for Europe in May 1902. When the Coronation was postponed by the King's illness, he travelled extensively: he was photographed in Edinburgh wearing impeccable morning dress and top hat. At the suggestion of the King himself – an expert on uniforms of all kinds – he was fitted with the full dress outfit of a British ambassador for the Coronation ceremony. He took it home, together with the morning dress to use for ceremonial occasions. Colin Harding, who accompanied the party, said that "in no single act did Lewanika or his staff commit an offence or even an indiscretion out of harmony with the traditional etiquette of either this or the country which gave them birth." And Lewanika said his greatest impression was of "the intelligence of the English people, and what the Gospel has done for them." But he never accepted the conversion to Christianity for which the missionaries had long sought. In the early days, even to give up his wives would have been to abandon a web of political alliances and to risk almost certain revolution. "If I am not converted, it is not your fault," he told Coillard. "You have given yourself no rest, but you do not give me any either." Now, though the fear of revolution had been removed, the experience of nine months' travel among people whose way of life was far different from that of the Paris Mission, the attraction had waned. And the saintly Coillard, his spiritual adviser for so long, died in 1904.

Ten years later, when the First World War broke out, Lewanika was over 70 years of age, and the conflict, with its threat of German invasion from the west, was a source of great anxiety to him. "Everybody feels as if they were in prison," he told a visitor. He was still tall and upright in 1915, his lined face imparting an impression of "great energy and a certain grandeur." But his health was failing, and he was frequently ill and confined to his house during his last three years. In January 1916, he took to his bed for the last time; he lapsed into unconsciousness early in February, and died peacefully at 11:30 on the night of 4 February.

His body was placed in the large canoe in which he always travelled, and crouched behind it was the chief mourner, Mawana Amatende, the wife who had gone with him into exile long before. Behind the canoe came the royal barge filled with all the King's possessions, both to be sunk in deep water after the burial, which took place in a vast, deep grave on Nanikelako, the mound on the flood plain of the Zambesi chosen by Lewanika himself. That night, the grave, now containing all the things the King would need in the next world – his fly-whisk, his karosses, his wooden bowls and earthenware pots – was filled in. Next day, a herd of 170 cattle was slaughtered on the grave.

His biographer wrote of him: "He died full of honour, loved and respected by his people as a great Chief, leaving the heart of his country reserved to the Barotse by treaty rights and his own family secure on the throne. No African ruler of his time achieved more, and none was more regretted by all who had known him."

78

THE WHITE CHIEF OF THE BEMBA

The Society of Missionaries of Africa is better known as the White Fathers, a French Roman Catholic order whose members formerly wore white tunics and hooded capes reflecting the Order's foundation in Algeria in 1868. The White Fathers came to Tanzania in 1878 and entered the country of the Mambwe, in what is now Zambia, in 1891. They moved after four years to Kayambi on the borders of the Bemba country. The party was led by Joseph Dupont, a French farmer's son, then 45 years old. Tall and white-bearded, he was a priest of commanding appearance and wide practical knowledge – farming and brick-making, carpentry and ironwork, medicine and chemistry. Now he had come to convert the Bemba to Christianity.

The Paramount Chief, Chitimukulu Sampa, opposed the White Fathers and in July 1895 sent men to kill Dupont. But when the saw him kill a guinea fowl for his supper with a single shot, they retreated in awe. And in 1897, Dupont scored a second triumph by apparently dispersing by exorcism the swarms of locusts which were devastating the land. One of the Chitimukulu's sons, Chief Makasa, who lived near Kayambi, was more favourably disposed towards the missionaries: he enjoyed disputing with Dupont and much admired the Fathers' good harvests. Among Makasa's people, Dupont gained the reputation of a sorcerer, and it is recorded that one day women came to Kayambi to sing the praises of the man they called "Moto Moto", Man of Fire:

> "This man is our chief.
> What parent loved his children as he does?
> Moto Moto, who helps poor people …
> He kills lions,
> He cures the sick.
> If you have seen another like him, tell us!"

In 1897, Fr. Dupont's pioneering work was recognised by the Pope, who made him Vicar Apostolic of Nyasa. He was now Bishop Dupont, and his episcopal coat of arms included a blazing fire to commemorate his Bemba nickname, Moto Moto. In 1898, Dupont was summoned by Chief Mwamba to his deathbed. Dupont could not save him, but made his last weeks more comfortable. At the end, Mwamba nominated Dupont as his heir and successor. Moto Moto, he said, was the only man who had ever dared look him straight in the face.

After Mwamba's death, Dupont proclaimed himself chief and persuaded a number of leading Bemba to sign a document which claimed Mwamba had given him "the whole of his country with the rights of the soil ... both the right of sovereignty over the whole country and territory and the special protection of his women and children." When called to account by Robert Codrington, the powerful, autocratic Administrator of North-Eastern Rhodesia, Dupont said he only wished to acquire a grant of land for a mission station in the Bemba heartland. Codrington dismissed Dupont's chiefly claim, but allowed him to take up a place near Mwamba's village for the propagation of Christianity.

Dupont was never truly recognised as a chief by the Bemba, who thought of him only as a regent, or by the civil administration of the British South Africa Company. But, as the historian Robert Rotberg has written, "the Bishop's intervention in the affairs of the Bemba, no matter how narrow the motive, helped to prevent bloodshed after the death of Mwamba and precipitated the assumption of British sovereignty for the first time over the central plateaux of North-Eastern Rhodesia ..."

Dupont, his health broken by malaria, was forced to leave Africa for Europe in 1900. Four years later, he returned to his beloved Bemba and stayed among them until 1911, when he was finally obliged to return to France. "Every fibre of my heart is fixed in Ubemba," he wrote; "to take it from me will finish me." But with his health restored, he lived another 20 years, and died among the White Fathers in Algeria in 1930, within sight of the little garden he called Malole after the place he had first chosen for his mission to the Bemba.

79

BUTALA BWA MAKA'S MUSEUM

The Moto Moto Museum at Mbala marks the extraordinary achievement of a French-Canadian missionary, Fr. Jean-Jacques Corbeil of the White Fathers, who began in 1956 to collect the things made by the Bemba people around him at Mulilansolo "just for the personal pleasure of knowing more about the people I was living among." More importantly, he collected "Mbusa," the sacred emblems used in the initiation of a Bemba girl when she reaches maturity. These initiation ceremonies are said to have begun in the time of Mukulumpe, father of the first Chitimukulu, paramount chief of all the Bemba, more than 500 years ago. The ceremonies and songs, which teach the young girls their family, domestic and social duties, and which include blessings and prayers, were kept secret from all men. In 1960, however, Fr. Corbeil began to persuade the people to reveal their ancient traditions so that they might be preserved for the future in times of rapid change. He recorded over 100 songs used in the initiations and collected many of the pottery models and the wall and floor paintings.

He became an expert on Bemba medicine, a collector not only of Mbusa but of Stone Age and Iron Age relics, of the tools and products of traditional industries, of symbols of royalty – anything that embraced the history and traditions of the old Zambia. And when Fr Corbeil was transferred to a mission at Serenje, he began another collection, and by his unlimited activities both as priest and collector, earned himself the name of "Butala bwa Maka" – "Mr. Energy." In 1972, his collections at last found a home in a former mechanical workshop 3km north-east of Mbala, and he named the museum "Moto Moto", Man of Fire, honouring the name the Bemba had given a century before to another White Father, Bishop Dupont, and, appropriately, the museum also contains relics of that pioneering missionary. The museum was given to the National Museums Board in 1973, and officially opened by Unia Mwila, then Minister for the Northern Province, on 27 April 1974. Extensions financed by overseas aid were completed in 1982 and officially opened by the then President

Fr. Jean-Jacques Corbeil, the French-Canadian missionary who learnt more about the Bemba than most Bemba knew, and collected 7 000 items for his museum – a unique achievement and a tribute to the trust placed in him by the people among whom he was living.

Kaunda in October 1983. Its collections total over 7 000 items.

In his book, "Mbusa," Fr. Corbeil wrote that "perhaps the greatest contribution which Zambia can give to the rest of the world is to be found in the traditional teaching of marriage and family life, particularly as expressed in the initiation ceremonies of girls and boys." His desire, he said, was to help the people of Zambia "keep alive a great love for a pride in their customs, and to remind them of the sacredness of family life and the obligations they undertake when they enter into marriage." Fr. Corbeil retired at last to his native Canada where he died in February 1990.

80

THE LITTLE GIANT

On August 22 1888, The Times newspaper in London published an extraordinary article of three columns headed "Great Britain's policy in Africa, by an African explorer." It was a brilliant and concise development of the policy of the Prime Minister, Lord Salisbury; it pointed to Africa as the new world of the 19th century as America had been to the 16th, and it foreshadowed the "Cape to Cairo" dream of Cecil Rhodes. The author of the article was 30 years of age, an unknown civil servant – Vice-Consul for the Cameroons – named Harry Hamilton Johnston, five feet and three inches of demonic energy and ambition: a man blessed with a dozen out-standing talents whose active life was by good fortune to coincide almost exactly with the international "Scramble for Africa." He was explorer, concession-hunter, treaty-maker, administrator, the archetype of the "man on the spot." But despite his brilliant achievements, he had to wait 30 years for a biographer – who explained that Johnston's misfortune was

A true polymath – Harry Hamilton Johnston, soldier, administrator, artist, author, linguist, and much else, commemorated in Zambia only by the undistinguished rapids on the Luapula near Mambilima, called the Johnston Falls.

that "he allowed his rich humour and his extravagant flights of fancy to flow freely on the most formal occasions and on the most serious subjects. He never knew the meaning of discretion ..." In public life, it was fatal to his career, and at the age of 43, he retired to the countryside with still a third of his life to live.

Johnston was born in London in 1858, the first in his father's twelve children by his second wife. In his 21st year, Harry Johnston abandoned the prospects of a distinguished career as an artist to become an active agent for the expansion of the British Empire. After earning his living as a traveller in Africa by his pen and brush, he obtained an appointment in the consular service and in 1889 became British Consul in Mozambique. With £2 000 obtained from Cecil Rhodes, he financed an expedition up the Zambesi, made treaties with a number of chiefs, and returned in 1891 as first Commissioner and Consul-General in Nyasaland. By agreement with the Foreign Office, he also received £10 000 a year from the British South Africa Company for the administration of North-Eastern Rhodesia.

Most of the next five years Johnston spent as a self-taught soldier in breaking the slave trade on Lake Nyasa and in the establishment of administrative posts in Nyasaland and in North-Eastern Rhodesia. His official "Report of the First Three Years' Administration of the Eastern Portion of British Central Africa", presented to Parliament in 1894 had to be reprinted several times: he discoursed on climate, geology, botany, zoology and the people of his colony. Those who distrusted Rhodes's ruthless and materialistic approach to Empire saw in Johnston a gentler and more rational creed of expansion, recognising the problems of administration. In 1895, when the last of the slavers had been defeated, the Company took over the administration of North-Eastern Rhodesia, and Johnston himself, his health ruined by malaria and three attacks of blackwater, was forced to leave Central Africa in 1896. In the New Year's honours of that year, he became, at 37, the youngest knight in the Empire. But Lord Salisbury had no job to offer him; though he had quarrelled with Rhodes, his association with that name after the Jameson Raid was fatal to his ambitions. He was posted to Tunis as Consul-General, a demotion of which he made the best by becoming a reclusive scholar and artist whose pictures were hung annually at the Royal Academy and whose books appeared at short intervals: his correspondence was with many of the eminent figures of the time.

In July 1899 he was offered a post as Special Commissioner in Uganda; the danger to his health was compared with an unusually generous salary, and he accepted it. His achievements there in administration and constitutional development were outstanding. On his return to

London, he was warmly welcomed, raised in the order of knighthood – but the effects of blackwater ruled him out of the tropics, and the Foreign Office ruled him as not one of them. The Treasury gave him a far from generous pension. He and his wife moved to the hamlet of Poling near Arundel in Sussex where he continued to lead a life of intense private activity. Among a remarkable output of books in this period, the outstanding one was his Comparative Study of the Bantu & Semi-Bantu Languages – a work of 1 350 pages dealing with 300 languages and dialects. But in 1925 he suffered a stroke, and after two years of frail health, a second one killed him in 1927. He was buried at Poling, where his tombstone is inscribed with a tribute from the Kabaka and people of Uganda: "His faithfulness to Buganda shows that England wishes all whom she protects to be free." In the church, a simple tablet describes him as administrator, soldier, explorer, naturalist, author and painter.

Curiously, his only memorial in Zambia is the naming, in 1892, by Alfred Sharpe, the Commissioner for British Central Africa, of the Johnston Falls on the Luapula River. These, more a series of rapids than a waterfall, became better known for the nearby mission of the same name on a site chosen by the pioneer missionary Dan Crawford in 1897. The mission is now called Mambilima, an outpost of the Christian Brethren whose schools and hospitals around Zambia care for the minds and bodies as well as the souls of those about them.

81

BWANA CHANGA CHANGA

Not so many years ago, it was common for any personnel manager or location superintendent on the Copperbelt to be called "Changa Changa", but few of the callers or the called knew why. It was, in fact, the name given to John Harrison Clark, one of the first white settlers in what is now Zambia. In his youth, Clark was tall and powerfully built and cultivated a fierce black moustache. He was born about 1860, the son of a respectable Port Elizabeth ironmonger. For reasons that only rumour can now relate – there was the tale of someone shot by a revolver which "went off accidentally" – he wandered north in search of obscurity and adventure. About 1887 he crossed the Zambesi from Mozambique at Feira, then in ruins, and drifted, apparently penniless, for hundreds of kilometres westward from the Zambesi to the Kafue, to the Ila country. He said that his providential arrival on the day of the death of an important chief led to his succession to the post and to powers and privileges of which he made full use.

Harrison Clark, the benevolent despot of the 1890s, sitting arrogantly on a leopard skin, tarboosh at a cocky angle, on the verandah of his fortress-like home, Algoa, where he said, he "flew the red ensign and put down the slave trade".

His name, Changa Changa, "The Clever One", became known far and wide: he drove off Portuguese slavers, collected "tax" from Arab traders coming in, issued licences, took every other tusk of ivory going out, and accumulated cattle. He kept his headquarters at Feira, married the daughter of Mpuka, Chief of the Chikunda, and in 1895 built himself a substantial home, built like a fort and stockaded, at the confluence of the Lukusashi and Lunsemfwa rivers north of Feira in what is now the Mkushi district. He called it Algoa, the Portuguese name for his home town, and it became famous: as late as 1922 The Times atlas gave Algoa the same prominence as Livingstone, the capital of Northern Rhodesia.

Clark made treaties with chiefs over a vast area and boasted he could raise an army of thousands. But the British South Africa Company's charter had been extended north of the Zambesi in 1891, and although it took seven years for the first police post to be opened – at Monze – trouble lay ahead for Clark. One of the chiefs with whom he had signed a treaty went all the way to Salisbury to complain of what he said were Clark's high-handed appropriations of grain, chickens, cattle and ivory as "tax" – and even one of his wives. In 1901, the Company established a boma at Feira. Clark backed down gracefully. He accepted three farms – including Algoa and a small area called Fiperere to which he moved about 1903, and Chingombe, now a mission. But the people still regarded Changa Changa as their ruler, and by the end of the decade he had been charged several times for holding a court without authority. By the end of the First World War, however, Clark had long been deprived of his old powers and he was struggling to make a living by recruiting labour for the mines of Southern Rhodesia, supplying flour to the recruitment agency at Feira, and even selling dried bananas from Chingombe, a fertile and well-watered area, but too far from the line of rail. He experimented with cotton, but was flooded out, tried rubber, but the rainfall was too low.

At last he gave up his farms and came into Broken Hill where the mine was struggling to survive on the production of lead. There he became a partner in the brewing and selling of chibuku for the whole mine area and, now at last reasonably prosperous, became a popular, well-dressed pillar of the town's society. He presented a gold medal for motorcycle racing, and as the owner of a Model T Ford, became one of the town's first motorists. He died on 9 December 1927, about 67 years of age. A few years later, his friends placed a drinking fountain in the town centre. It bore the inscription "To the Memory of the Pioneer J. Harrison Clark (Changa Changa)." It has long since gone, erasing one of the last material links with a man whose strange, romantic life linked the old Africa with the new.

82

CHIRUPULA

John Edward Stephenson was 20 in 1896 when he left his job as a telegraphist in his native Sunderland and set out for adventure in Africa. He arrived in Blantyre via Kimberley and Bulawayo to work for the Africa Transcontinental Telegraph Company, founded by Rhodes to link the Cape with Cairo – but it never got beyond Ujiji. In Blantyre, Stephenson met his first wife, an Ngoni girl called Loti, for whom he paid ten shillings. She followed him to the newly-established capital of North-Eastern Rhodesia, Fort Jameson, where, in 1900, he transferred to the District Administration.

In July of that year, he was sent on an expedition, led by Francis Jones and accompanied by a tame baboon, to establish government in the Hook of the Kafue. Chirupula always claimed that the warm welcome the

Chirupula, the romantically-minded Sunderland telegraphist who founded the first Ndola, cut the track that became the Great North Road, wrote an autobiography, attracted a biographer – a kind and gentle eccentric despite the name that meant "He Who Beats Hard."

expedition received was because they were recognised as the founders of the tribe come back to earth – Kashindika who owned the West, Luchere who owned the East, and Shingo, who usually took the form of a lion, but could change into any animal. Jones, Stephenson and the baboon fitted the legend neatly.

Stephenson went on to found the boma at Mkushi and to earn his name Chirupula ("He Who Beats Hard") – strange for one remembered as gentle, but earned when corporal punishment was commonplace and began in early schooldays – and it certainly did not deter the Lala chief Chiwali from suggesting his own daughter, Mwape, as a wife for Stephenson. In 1904, Stephenson was promoted and sent to found the first Ndola, 11km from its present site. But now aligning himself with the ruled rather than with the rulers, he quarrelled with his superiors over the raising of poll tax and the boundaries of Lewanika's kingdom, and resigned. For less than £100 be bought 1 000 acres in a valley south-east of the Irumi Hills in the Mkushi district and built his first home, Chiwefwe, "The Place of Warmth."

Here at first he earned a precarious living recruiting labour for Broken Hill mine and guiding travellers to the Belgian Congo. When the railway connection was made in 1909, he found modest prosperity through planting citrus orchards, and there is a photograph of him standing proudly by a box of oranges punningly labelled "Chirupula – Beats All." By the mid-1920s he was the head of a household of two wives and eight children. Some of their names were a reflection of Chirupula's fanciful turn of mind – Alpha and Omega, Horatio, Torfrida, Otto and Ossa John. He also gave shelter to an increasing number of orphans – some of them probably the children of his ne'er-do-well brother Peter. It was an establishment which for many years meant isolation from the conventional white society of Broken Hill.

Realignment of the Great North Road made it more difficult to get his fruit from orchard to market along an increasingly rutted track; Loti left him, and in what he described as "a kind of emotional exhaustion" he sent Mwape home to her father's village where, in 1934, she died. Alone, Stephenson began writing "Chirupula's Tale," a romantic version of his early years in Africa which, with its florid, eccentric prose patiently edited, was published in 1937. About this time, Chirupula gave shelter to six Jewish refugees from Hitler, and after war broke out, provided help and hospitality to many of the troops passing up and down the Great North Road to and from East Africa.

But the war years brought several crop failures and a serious decline in his fortunes. He had to sell much of his farm and move to

"Stonehenge," a thatched house of his own eccentric design a short distance away at Kapiri Muwandika. In 1946, Chirupula turned 70 and dedicated himself more to publicising his conviction of the Egyptian origins of the Bantu people. He pressed his theory on the public through "Chirupula's Gazette," a duplicated quarterly which mixed his own brand of Egyptology with anecdotes of his early days and attacks on Government policy which he backed with streams of rambling argument composed on an ancient typewriter and posted to successive Governors.

Despite Stonehenge's isolation, Chirupula's reputation had been spread by travellers on the Great North Road who had enjoyed his hospitality, his ebullient personality and his wealth of anecdote. They included troops travelling through in wartime, General Smuts on a botanical expedition in 1930, and hundreds of casual callers. His fame spread further in 1951 with the publication of a biography written by the American Kathaleen Stevens, daughter of an early general manager of Broken Hill mine. Its title, "Jungle Pathfinder", is a strong clue to its dramatisation of Chirupula's exploits. By the time of the Rhodes Centenary Exhibition in Bulawayo in 1953, he merited treatment as an important visitor and as one of the few surviving links with the pioneering past - and he revelled in it.

Old age and illness brought him at last to a hospital bed in Lusaka, and when it became clear there could be no recovery, he was taken home, where he died on 15 August 1957 at the age of 81. He was buried near his home, wrapped in reed mats in Lala fashion, covered with a Union Jack, with a parson's prayers and a Masonic service. There were hundreds present – his children and grandchildren, crowds of Lala, many of whom had kept vigil all the night before – and even the Mayor of Broken Hill and the Deputy Provincial Commissioner representing the Governor.

They were celebrating the long life of a man of eccentric spirit, but of innocent charm, kindness and generosity which had won him a thousand friends and left him without an enemy.

83

YENGWE AND THE HOSPITAL

*V*ery few Zambians under the age of 50 will know why a hospital on a magnificent site in North Rise, Ndola, was named after Arthur Davison. Who on earth was he? He was a well-known character in the early days of Northern Rhodesia. He was born in County Durham, England, in 1882, and came to Africa with the Cleveland Bridgebuilding Co. at the age of 22 to work on the Victoria Falls bridge. It was at this time that he earned his name "Yengwe", derived from the Zulu word Ingeinyama, lion. He was travelling on a rail trolley when he came across a pride of lions sunning themselves on the track. Davison innocently threw stones at them to move them on. Fortunately, they moved on. During the next half century, Yengwe worked in many places – Zaire, Angola, Mozambique as well as Northern Rhodesia – at many occupations – prospecting, mining, farming, contracting and soldiering – in the First World War in East Africa, in the Second in Ethiopia despite being 57 years old in 1939. He was, however, extremely fit, a keen boxer in his youth who maintained the habits of training and never touched alcohol or tobacco in his life.

Yengwe, or "Ginger Dick" as he was also affectionately known, had a passion for land and strange houses. He had a farm near Bwana Mkubwa on which he began to build, but never completed, a shapeless mansion. This he left in his will to found a blind school, and at Solwezi, land for a Boy Scout camp, at Ndola a house to found a home for old men. He built a house on the beach on Lake Tanganyika, but got his levels wrong. When the bath plug was pulled out, the lake ran in. This house was abandoned because of sleeping sickness, and Yengwe plagued Government for years with claims for compensation.

But the most spectacular of his homes was at North Rise, Ndola, and not only because of its position, dominating the landscape of eastern Ndola and commanding splendid views. It was four stories tall, a random mass of concrete totally without architectural merit, and soon known as "Davison's Castle." Around it, the rubble of unfinished extensions did duty for a garden. On the third floor, a door led not to a new wing but,

Arthur Davison, whose monstrous concrete castle, built on one of the finest sites in Ndola, had to be dynamited to make way for the children's hospital which bears his name.

unnerving to the unfamiliar visitor, to nothing. The soil pipe for the plumbing descended through the centre of the upstairs sitting room which he had decorated with swords, shields and other booty from his Ethiopian war service as an experienced and enterprising quartermaster. At his death, at the age of 74, in 1955, he left the castle and its nine-acre site to the Roman Catholic Church to build a hospital. Originally it was to have been built by public subscription and to be run by Irish nuns for Europeans, Asians and Coloureds – for this was during Federation. These plans died a natural death, and after the monstrous concrete castle was demolished by dynamite, Davison's name was attached to a hospital built for children – any child, all children.

84

RHODES'S YOUNG MEN

Frederick Arnot, the first Christian missionary in what was to become Zambia, lived at Lealui from 1882 to 1884, and during this time persuaded King Lewanika to form an alliance with King Khama of the Ngwato, who favoured co-operation with the British, rather than with Lobengula, King of the Matabele, who wanted allies in a war to drive the white men out. In 1891, Lewanika asked for British protection, but he had a long wait for it to arrive. The Matabele War of 1893 and the rebellion of 1896 occupied the British South Africa Company so much that it was 1897 before Rhodes was able to send Major Robert Coryndon with a small escort – and a portrait of Queen Victoria for Lewanika – from Bulawayo to Lealui.

Coryndon was then 27 years old, son of one of Rhodes's old Kimberley friends, and one of the so-called "Young Lambs", or "Twelve Apostles", a dozen men of varied talents that Rhodes gathered about him. Coryndon had been a trooper in the 1890 Pioneer Column which had occupied Southern Rhodesia, he had fought in both the Matabele War and the Rebellion, and rose to the rank of major. In January 1897 he had accompanied Rhodes to London as his secretary for the Jameson Raid inquiry and toured Europe with him after it. He had at first resisted appointment as Rhodes's secretary. "That's not my job, sir," he said. "Think of something I am suited for!" Rhodes found it. A few months later, Rhodes sent Coryndon to persuade Lewanika to grant the Company new powers to extend the administration within his kingdom. Coryndon got on well with King Lewanika, and in 1898 he conceded administrative, mining, and commercial rights in return for an annual subsidy and the reservation of large tracts of land to the Lozi people.

The territory now claimed by the Company was so vast and communications so poor that in the early years it was divided in two across its narrowest part. For Lewanika's country, the North-West, Rhodes chose Coryndon because his charm, courage and natural skill as a diplomatist were well suited to leading a small party to negotiate with a powerful

Robert Codrington, the brusque, tough, brilliant administrator, but with a fatally weakened heart that killed him at 39.

king. Coryndon was also a man of impressive physical strength. Sir Cecil Rodwell – a trustworthy witness – said Coryndon "could tear in half a new pack of cards, tear the half in half, and then the quarter in half." He was a great lover of the veld, a fine shot and a keen naturalist. He was not so well suited to administration, however, and his achievements in this field were limited, though he did arrange the first weekly postal service to the south, reorganised the police force, and moved Livingstone from the Old Drift to its present site.

He was happier out hunting with his mule-drawn buckboard wagon. A contemporary recalled that one night in camp, a hyena slunk up, seized him by the hand and pulled him from his blankets. Coryndon fought off the hyena, bandaged his hand, waited for it to return, and shot it. Lord Selborne, the British High Commissioner in South Africa, recognised Coryndon's talents and sent him to Swaziland to straighten out that protectorate's troubled affairs. He went on to Basutoland and to the successive governorships of Uganda and Kenya, where he died as Sir Robert Coryndon in 1925.

For the North-East, which at first was administered by the Imperial Commissioner, Harry Johnston, from what is now Malawi, Rhodes chose another of his young men. Robert Codrington was something of an opposite to Coryndon, a man of brusque manner and great administrative talent. He was born in 1869 of a naval family, but joined the Bechuanaland Border Police in 1890. In 1893, as a sergeant-major, he was

Robert Coryndon the courageous soldier and skilful diplomat who negotiated with Lewanika in 1898. He died in 1925 as Sir Robert Coryndon, Governor of Kenya.

wounded while riding with the great hunter, Selous, to rescue a party ambushed in the war against Lobengula. He joined Harry Johnston in the administration of Nyasaland in 1895, and fought the Ngoni in 1896 and the Yao in 1897. On holiday in England in 1898, he so impressed Rhodes that he made him Deputy Administrator of North-Eastern Rhodesia – perhaps because he set his own salary at £800 a year, about £50 000 in today's money. Rhodes, taken aback for once, said: "That seems rather a large amount." "Well," said Codrington, "I'm worth it, and I won't go for less." He got the job.

He became Administrator in 1900, travelled widely round his territory and made many improvements to the standard of living and health of his officials. His gruff manner, bordering on rudeness, earned him his African name "Mara" – it is settled – the curt ending he put to any argument. But he was noted for his relatively advanced readiness to employ Africans as clerks and telegraphists, and as one of the first serious collectors of ethnographic material in Central Africa. In 1907, his reputation won him promotion as successor to Coryndon as Administrator of North-Western Rhodesia – a post rapidly gaining in importance with the arrival of the railway line. Codrington acted with his usual decisiveness, sacking unsuitable men, moving the capital from fever-ridden Kalomo to Livingstone, riding his old hobby-horse of improving housing to cut malaria, and introducing his North-Eastern administrative system so that the amalgamation of the two territories into Northern Rhodesia in 1911 went smoothly.

But Codrington did not live to see it. Though tall and powerfully built, he suffered like his master Rhodes with serious heart trouble, probably weakened by malaria and strenuous living. He sailed home for marriage to Miss Dorothie Bird, daughter of Sir Alfred Bird of custard fame, only to drop dead outside his London hotel in December 1908. He was only 39. His ethnographic collection, housed in the National Museum of Zimbabwe in Bulawayo, remains a tangible memorial to his life and times.

85

THE GENTLEMAN ADVENTURER

George Grey was born in 1866 at Fallodon in Northumberland, the estate of a family distinguished in its service to the British crown and government. His grandfather was the Liberal statesman Sir George Grey, his father, Col. George Grey, was equerry to the Prince of Wales, his eldest brother became Viscount Grey and Secretary of State for Foreign Affairs. In 1891, when he was 25, George Grey arrived in Africa to work for a mining syndicate in Southern Rhodesia. He fought in the Matabele War of 1893 and in the 1896 Rebellion he raised and trained his own unit which achieved considerable fame as Grey's Scouts. When peace returned, he went back to prospecting and mining, and when Robert Williams formed

Tanganyika Concessions to prospect along the Katanga border in 1899, he sent Grey "on a pure adventure" as he called it, to check reports of extensive ancient mine workings and a trade in copper crosses and bars.

On this first expedition, Grey pegged what was to become Chambishi Mine and investigated the extensive ancient workings at Kansanshi. In his second expedition to the north in 1901 – after spending a few months' on active service in the Boer War – he went on to discover the vast copper deposits of Katanga. It was a large, well-equipped expedition which set out from Bulawayo with 12 ox wagons, 200 pack donkeys and mules,

George Grey: but for a disabling stammer, he might have matched the highest achievements of his distinguished family. As it was, he became best known for heroic feats of bicycling through the bush.

and riding horses. But tsetse fly killed virtually all the animals, and only one wagon reached Kansanshi six months later: the rest of the stores were on the heads of 1 000 carriers. On the strength of Grey's reports, Williams obtained a mining concession from King Leopold of the Belgians and Grey spent the next five years overcoming the difficulties of developing the Katanga mines far from the nearest supply base.

It was at this time, 1901 to 1906, that Grey, as manager, achieved fame among his contemporaries for his extraordinary journeys by bicycle. The best-known of these feats of endurance was when Grey was at Kambove and Robert Williams sent word from London that he was to close down Kansanshi mine; Grey knew that for security he had to have it as a base in British territory, and he decided to make his case in person, in London, and set off on his cycle. On the first day he cycled from Kambove to Kansanshi, about 150km. The next day he cycled another 150km, camping near Kasempa. On the third day he covered half the distance between Kasempa and Ninga (near present-day Mumbwa). On the fourth evening, he reached Ninga, headquarters of the Northern Copper Co., where Tom Davey, discoverer of Broken Hill Mine, found him dressed in shirtsleeves, cut-down breeches "such as Boy Scouts wear", and carrying only a razor, a toothbrush "and a tin of Plasmon biscuits." He refused Davey's offer of a revolver: "Every ounce of weight counts," Grey said. The following day, Grey made the drift at Kafue and on the evening of the sixth day he cycled into Kalomo. After a day's rest, he cycled on the eighth day to the Victoria Falls where he hired a Cape cart to drive him south to the construction railhead. He arrived in England 33 days after leaving Kambove.

Grey regularly cycled the 150km between Kambove and Ruwe, leaving at 4am and arriving before 4pm. The nearest telegraph office was at Abercorn, which the Africa Trans-Continental Telegraph had reached in 1899. The distance is about 700km, and needing to send an important cable, he cycled there and back with a two-day rest between. When the railway reached Broken Hill in January 1906, Grey decided to attempt smelting of high-grade oxide ores at Kansanshi, and a small blast furnace was taken from railhead to the mine: two years later it was the first commercial producer of copper in Northern Rhodesia.

But by this time, Grey had left Tanganyika Concessions because, he said, he was "getting into a groove." His restless nature made him turn down an office job and reject the idea of ranching. He settled for an appointment as Special Commissioner in Swaziland, making sense of what he called a nightmare of ill-judged concessions to white men, often for the same land and for conflicting purposes. It took him two years, but at the end he said with justifiable pride that "I have been the instrument that has locked up much beautiful, fertile country from which the whites are to be excluded." Lord Selborne said he doubted if, in the history of the British Empire, there had been a more tiresome and intricate piece of administrative work. In 1911, Grey was hunting on horeseback in Kenya when, in a rare occurrence, an unwounded lion charged him. He dismounted and got off two quick shots, but they were not fatal, and the lion mauled him severely. He died in Nairobi a few days later at the age of 45.

In so short a life he had been the instrument of the discovery of both the Zambian and Zairean copperbelts. He had also won from the great hunter Selous the opinion that he was "one of the finest specimens of an Englishman in the country – quiet, self-contained and unassuming, but at the same time, brave, capable and energetic." With all these heroic virtues, Grey suffered from a bad stammer, and struggled to master it all his life. It has been said that but for the stammer, he would have risen to great heights in any career he chose. Perhaps in the frustration caused by that knowledge lay his restlessness. In 1916, a tablet made of Katanga copper and bearing a faithful cast of his features was unveiled in St. John's Church, Bulawayo, by the Administrator, Drummond Chaplin. It said that "for his great and rare qualities he was trusted, followed, held in honour and loved by all who worked with or for him …"

86

Sikorski's Tourists

The ancient kingdom of Poland, carved up between Russia, Germany and Austria in the 18th century, was put together again at the end of the First World War. But it proved a brief interlude of independence. The Poles became the first victims of the Second World War. In September 1939, they found themselves squeezed between the conflicting ambitions of Hitler in the West and Stalin in the East. Polish soldiers and civilians alike became refugees in hundreds of thousands, fleeing both armies into Hungary and Romania. A Polish government in exile was formed by Wladyslaw Sikorski, a heroic soldier-statesman. Hitler sneered that the vast and tragic hordes of refugees were "Sikorski's tourists."

A fortunate few hundred of them, men, women and children who had fled from Romania into Turkey, obtained British protection and were moved first to Cyprus and then to Palestine. The men were mostly professional people – lawyers, scientists, civil servants; many, especially the Jews among them, were in particular danger from the Germans. As the war in the Middle East grew more threatening, a more permanent settlement was sought for them: the Government of Northern Rhodesia was asked to provide one. The first group of 282 left the Middle East on 21 July 1941, disembarked at Durban and arrived by train at Livingstone on 7 August. Major Hugh McKee, a well-known Lusaka businessman and member of the Legislative Council, was appointed the first Officer in Charge of Camps and War Evacuees. Most of the new arrivals were settled at Livingstone, a few were distributed among Monze, Mazabuka, Kafue and Lusaka. A small group was sent to Fort Jameson. Most were given hotel rooms paid for by government, a few families were privately billetted. They were given small monthly living allowances and pocket money for the children. A few dozen found jobs.

At the beginning of 1943, the situation changed. Eighteen thousand Polish refugees were sent to Africa. They had survived fearful hardships in Soviet labour camps, been driven across Europe into Persia – men, many of them old or wounded, together with women and children, most of them ill, all of them half-starved. By the end of 1944, 3 000 of the Persian group had arrived in Northern Rhodesia. With so many, there was no hope of hotel rooms or private houses. Lt-Col. Stewart Gore-Browne, also a member of Legco, succeeded McKee in caring for the refugees and was committed to a programme of building camps to house them. The first of them, just off what is now Addis Ababa Drive in Lusaka, opened in February 1943 with 534 women, 85 men and 313 children under the age of 16. At Bwana Mkubwa, the Rhokana Corporation leased 200 acres to Government for a camp holding 490 women, 190 men and 385 children. The third camp was established at Abercorn in the far north. Its refugees – 274 women, 93 men and 212 children, were brought from Kigoma on Lake Tanganyika by a Belgian steamer. The fourth camp was the small one which had at first housed refugees from the Cyprus group at Fort Jameson: it held 43 women, seven men and five children brought by road from Lusaka. Each of these camps was provided with a farm on which to grow food for the refugees – Rietvlei at Lusaka, Kombowa at Bwana Mkubwa, Nakatali for Abercorn and Katapola for Fort Jameson.

The Polish government in exile had an office in Nairobi which appointed camp leaders, and with elected camp councils and advisory committees, the camps became largely self-governing. Indeed, in September 1944 a fifth camp was opened – a penal settlement at Katombora, west of Livingstone, which at one time held eleven men, five women and a girl. But Government decided after a while that it must retain ultimate judicial power and the Katombora camp was closed early in 1945. A few months later, in May 1945, the war in Europe ended, with Poland occupied by the Soviet army and doomed to decades of Communist dictatorship. The British Government allowed the Polish refugees to decide for themselves whether or not they wished to return to their homeland. Slowly they were dispersed until the last of the camps was closed in 1948. For the most part, the Poles in Northern Rhodesia went to Britain. Some went to America, Europe or Australia. A few stayed to see Northern Rhodesia become Zambia, to make their mark in many different fields and to add strange, unpronounceable names to the telephone directory. Time has carried most of them away, and little now remains even of the small monuments built by the refugees at Bwana Mkubwa and Abercorn to remind Zambia of the part it played in giving thousands of victims of war a new beginning.

EPILOGUE

One lifetime could span the entire colonial history of Zambia. A man born in 1889, when the British South Africa Company was granted its royal charter, could comfortably live until 1964 and see the Union Jack come down. In the perspective of human history, a hundred years is but the blinking of an eye, but to those who look back from the 1990s, the century just past seems an aeon of profound change. It carved from the undisturbed forests and hills, without regard for much except the politics of a few European countries, a kidney-shaped colony. Upright young Englishmen – preferably from public school – drilled in the concept of duty and service in the cause of Empire were recruited to drive off the slavers, introduce money – and tax it – build roads and bomas, and exercise authority. They were preceded, accompanied and followed by a service of another kind – that which was moved by a powerful precept: "Go ye, therefore, and teach all nations ..." These were the missionaries whose faith and zeal sought to bring the blessings and knowledge of Christianity to the heart of Africa.

These pioneers of colonialism were, with the exceptions that humankind must contain, men and women of good will (even if later generations regard them as misguided), and there is an anecdote in which may be seen the virtues of both the temporal and the spiritual powers. The tale concerns Willie Lammond, a missionary who came to Africa on a ship which, near their landing in Angola, passed another carrying slaves to work the cocoa plantations of the islands off the Guinea coast. The year was 1900, and Willie walked in: there was, as he said, no Lobito, no railway, no wheeled traffic, no road into the interior, only the paths trodden bare by the feet of countless slaves.

His destination was the Johnston Falls Mission (now called Mambilima) on the Luapula River in the land of Mwata Kazembe, king of the Lunda, who had his capital near the south end of Lake Mweru. It was from the lips of Henry Pomeroy, who had begun to build the mission in 1898, that Lammond heard the tale of the king and the missionary ...

In 1899, the Administrator, Robert Codrington, despatched a punitive force against Kazembe for what he claimed were "repeated acts of aggression." He was wrong – it was the Arab slavers who were fighting for the survival of their infamous trade, and Kazembe repeatedly sought British protection because he was powerless against them. Now, in the face of a machine gun, the king saw that argument or resistance were useless, and he fled across the Luapula with the Arabs. Two weeks later, he came to Johnston Falls with the remainder of his followers.

"Mrs. Anderson, sister to Mr. Pomeroy, managed to persuade him to return and meet the Europeans by promising to accompany him and intercede for him with the officer in charge … As one of the officers said to me: 'What could we do with the man when a woman brought him by the hand and said 'Do be kind to him'?"

Mwata Kazembe was reinstated, still a powerful symbol of traditional life, culture and authority. He returned to his capital after what had proved to be the last armed demonstration by the Chartered Company in North-Eastern Rhodesia: the power of the Arab slavers had been broken, their hold over the chiefs was at an end, and a new era began.

In this simple anecdote may be seen the beginnings of Zambia. The arrogance of Victorian colonialism modified by the precepts of the Christian gospel, the overthrow of the cruelties of the slave trade, the beginnings of a modern administration in a new country, the imposition of law and order, the spread of education. But as the land and people were opened to new ways, minds were opened too, and the yearning for another kind of freedom – freedom from an alien domination – grew year by year. The historian Philip Mason expressed it memorably. "There is a level of consciousness at which men go about their work, eat their meals; laugh, dance and drink; tell the boss they have no complaints – and mean it. There may in the same men be another level, of which they are most of the time unaware, at which there is a deep, perpetual and bitter resentment. But at an emotional summons of a particular kind, this may leap into view …" The summons came from Harry Nkumbula and Kenneth Kaunda, prompted and sharpened by the imposition of Federation. By the exercise of common sense and common humanity, independence came in peace and harmony, with the last colonial governor handing over to the first republican president at a happy, uplifting ceremony.

At the end of the year 1999, Zambia will have been independent for 35 years, half the length of its colonial history. Let us hope the third millenium will bring new Tales of Zambia, to be recorded as these were, with the intention of enabling Zambians to understand the past, to enjoy the present, and to look forward to the future.

Sources

1. Zambia, the First Two Minutes: Republic of Zambia: Independence Celebrations: Detailed Working Programme, 22nd October to 28th October 1964. (Government Printer, Lusaka 1964).

2. The Flag, the Arms, the Anthem: Mrs. Gabriel Ellison, Lusaka; Mrs. Mererid Scott, Aberystwyth; Mr. J. Fairhurst, OBE, Cambridge (in litt.); Anthem Has Solid Claim to Being National (Sunday Times, Johannesburg, 31 October 1993); N.S. Ferris (ed): Know Your Rhodesia & Know Nyasaland (RP&P, Salisbury SR 1964); The Northern Rhodesia Handbook (2nd ed. Government Printer 1953); Zambia Today (Government Printer, Lusaka, 1964); Rotberg, Robert I.: The Rise of Nationalism in Central Africa (Harvard UP, 1965).

3. The People of Zambia: Brelsford, W.V.: The Tribes of Zambia (Government Printer, Lusaka, 1965); Johnston, H.H.: British Central Africa (Methuen 1897); Roberts, Andrew: A History of Zambia (Longman, 1976); Fagan, Brian M.: Early Farmers and Traders North of the Zambesi (in Oliver, Roland [ed]) The Middle Age of African History (OUP 1967); Langworthy, H.W.: Zambia Before 1890 (Longman 1972).

4. The Indispensable Element: Hobson, Dick: Horizon, magazine of the RST Group, July 1963.

5. Our Only Port: NR Journal Vol. 4 p.289; Simposya, Fred: Times of Zambia 1 August 1995.

6. Ndola's Sunken Lakes: Bell-Cross, G. Sunken Lakes in the Ndola District (NR Journal, Vol.4 p.433); Doke, C.M.: The Lambas of Northern Rhodesia (Harrap 1931).

7. The Kalambo Falls: NR Journal, Vol. 1, No.6 p.73.

8. Lake Bangweulu: Brelsford, W.V.: The Story of a Swamp (Horizon, magazine of the RST Group, July 1961); Crawford, D.: Thinking Black (Morgan & Scott, 1912); Debenham, Frank: Study of an African Swamp (HMSO 1952); Hughes, J.E.: Eighteen Years on Lake Bangweulu (The Field, ca. 1932); Holmes, Timothy (ed): David Livingstone, Letters & Documents 1841–1872 (James Currey, London 1990).

9. Musi-o-Tunya: Phillipson, D.W. (ed): Mosi-oa-Tunya: a handbook to the Victoria Falls Region (Longman 1975); Clark, J. Desmond (ed): The Victoria Falls: a handbook to the Victoria Falls, the Batoka Gorge & part of the upper Zambesi river (Commission for the Preservation of Natural & Historical Monuments & Relics, Lusaka 1952); Brelsford, W.V.: The Tribes of Zambia (Government Printer, Lusaka, 1965).

10. Getting Out of the Water: Prins, Gwyn: The Hidden Hippopotamus (Cambridge UP, 1980; Clay, Gervas: Your Friend, Lewanika (Chatto & Windus, 1978: No. 7 in the Robins Series, National Museum of Zambia); MacConnachie, John: An Artisan Missionary on the Zambesi (Oliphant, Anderson & Ferrier, ca. 1930).

11. Where the Rivers Meet: NR Journal Vol.2 No.5 pp75–77; Vol. 3 p. 92; Vol.4 pp 63–71, 399, 454–461, 493–5, 609; Vol.5 pp294–5,620; Vol.6 pp109–111, 275–292.

12. Kariba: Hobson, Dick: Kariba (unpublished typescript, 1961, revised 1970); Zambia Mining Year Book 1975 (Copper Industry Service Bureau, Kitwe, 1976); Clements, Frank: Kariba (Methuen, 1959); Morrell, David: Indictment (Faber & Faber 1987).

13. The Zambesi: Clark, J.D.: Origin & Spelling of the Name Zambezi (NR Journal, Vol.1, No.6, p. 69); Clark, J.D. (ed): The Victoria Falls Handbook (Commission for the Preservation of Natural & Historical Monuments & Relics, Lusaka 1952); D.W. Phillipson (ed): Mosi-oa-Tunya: A Handbook to the Victoria Falls Region (Longman, London, 1975); Venables, Bernard: Coming Down the Zambesi (Constable, 1974); Anon: River of a Nation (Horizon, magazine of the RST Group, March 1965);

Jeal, Tim: Livingstone (Heinemann, 1973).

14. Kazungula, the Meeting Point: First, Ruth: South West Africa (Penguin Africa Library, 1963); Trollope, Major L.F.W.: The Eastern Caprivi Zipfel (NR Journal Vol.3 p. 107); Craig, Prof. J.I.: Varsity Corner (Times of Zambia 19–21 May 1970.)

15. War on Lake Tanganyika: Shankland, Peter: The Phantom Flotilla (Collins, 1968); Tasker, George S.: Naval Occasions on Lake Tanganyika (NR Journal, Vol.3, p.57); Miller, Charles: Battle for the Bundu (Macdonald 1974).

16. Lake Mweru: Roberts, A.D.: A History of the Bemba (Longman, 1973); Sampson, Richard: They Came to Northern Rhodesia (Government Printer, Lusaka, 1961); Gould, Jeremy: Luapula: Dependence or Development? (Zambia Geographical Association, Finland, 1989); Graham, Ivor M.: A Quarrel at Lake Mweru (NR Journal, Vol.4, p.552); Baxter, T.W. (NR Journal, Vol. 3, p.82; Gore-Browne, S.: The Anglo-Belgian Boundary Commission, 1911–14 (NR Journal Vol.5 p.315); Clough, Eric: Chiengi: Some Notes (NR Journal, Vol.6, p.240); Brelsford, W.V.: Notes (NR Journal, Vol.6, p.104).

17. Kapenta: Jackson, P.B.N.: The Fishes of Northern Rhodesia (Government Printer, Lusaka, 1961); Skaife, Dr. S.H.: Mpulungu & Its Fisheries. (NR Journal, Vol.2, No.4, pp. 9–12); Anon: The Night Fishermen of Lake Tanganyika (Horizon, magazine of the RST Group, April 1965); Sikapizya Eleenson: letter (Times of Zambia, 14 July 1993).

18. Lechwe: Smithers, Reay H.N.: The Mammals of the Southern African Subregion. (University of Pretoria, 1983); Smith, E.W., & Dale, A.M.: The Ila-Speaking People of Northern Rhodesia (Macmillan, 1920); Vesey-Fitzgerald, Desmond: The Black Lechwe & Modern Methods of Wild Life Conservation (N.R. Journal, Vol.2, No.6, pp25–32).

19. Tiger Fish: Jackson, P.B.N.: The Fishes of Northern Rhodesia (Government Printer, Lusaka, 1961); Venables, Bernard: Coming Down the Zambesi (Constable, London, 1974); Tredgold, Sir Robert: The Rhodesia that was my Life (Allen & Unwin 1968).

20. White Ants: Scannell, Ted: The Teeming World of the Termite (Horizon, magazine of the RST group, February 1961); Storrs, A.E.G.: Know Your Trees (Forest Dept, Ndola, 1979); Duff, C.E.: Bashing the Bush (NR Journal Vol.2, No.1, p65); Pinhey, Elliott, & Loe, Ian: A Guide to the Insects of Zambia (Anglo American Corp. CA, 1973); Hughes, J.E.: Eighteen Years on Lake Bangweulu (The Field, London, ca.1932); Daily Telegraph, 23 March 1995: Flatulent Termites Cast a Cloud over the World.

21. Chembe, the Fish Eagle: Hughes, J.E.: Eighteen Years on Lake Bangweulu (The Field, London, ca. 1932); Mackworth-Praed, C.W. & Grant, C.H.B.: Birds of the Southern Third of Africa (Longmans, 1962); Benson, C.W. & White, C.M.N.: Check List of the Birds of Northern Rhodesia (Government Printer, Lusaka, 1957); Selous, F.C.: A Hunter's Wanderings in Africa (Richard Bentley, London, 1881); Benson, C.W., Brooke, R. K., Dowsett R.J., & Irwin, M.P.S.: The Birds of Zambia (Collins, London, 1971.

22. A Fine Fish: Jackson, P.B.N.: The Fishes of Northern Rhodesia (Government Printer, Lusaka, 1961); Kenmuir, Dale: Fishes of Kariba (Longmans, Zimbabwe, 1983); O'Donovan, D.: Angling for Tilapia in Northern Rhodesia (in NR Journal, Vol.3, p.397).

23. The Years of the Locust: Gunn, Dr. D.L.: The Story of the International Red Locust Control Service (Rhodesia Agricultural Journal, Vol.54, No.1, 1957); Gunn, Dr. D.L.: The Red Locust (Royal Society of Arts, London, 1952); Faure, Jacobus C.: The Life History of the Red Locust (Dept. of Agriculture, South Africa, 1935; Yule, William N.: The Eighth Plague (Shell Aviation News, July 1959); Hubbard, Wynant Davis: Ibamba

(Gollancz, London, 1962); Hobson, Dick: Showtime (Agricultural & Commercial Society of Zambia, Lusaka, 1979).

24. A Dose of Fever: Watson, Sir Malcolm: African Highway (John Murray, London, 1953); Hobson, Dick: Show Time (Agricultural & Commercial Society of Zambia, 1979); Roan Consolidated Mines Ltd: Zambia's Mining Industry – the First 50 Years (Ndola, 1978); Hobhouse, Henry: Seeds of Change (Harper & Row, New York, 1985); Lyell, D.D.: Hunting Trips in Northern Rhodesia (Horace Cox, London, 1910).

25. Nsulu, the Honey Guide: Mackworth-Praed, C.W., & Grant, C.H.B.: Birds of the Southern Third of Africa (Longman 1962); Carr, Norman: The White Impala (Collins, 1969); Hughes, J.E.: Eighteen Years on Lake Bangweulu (The Field, London, ca. 1932).

26. Kafue National Park: Clarke, John, & Loe, Ian: A Guide to the National Parks of Zambia (Anglo American Corp. CA, Lusaka, 1974); Hobson, R.H.: The Kafue National Park (unpublished ms, 1956); Hudson, J.W.H. (in litt.).

27. The Baobab Tree: Carr, Norman: Some Common Trees & Shrubs of the Luangwa Valley (Wildlife Conservation Society of Zambia ca. 1975); Storrs, A.E.G.: Know Your Trees (Forest Dept., Ndola, 1979); NR Journal, Vol.1, No.2, p.73; Hughes, J.E.: Eighteen Years on Lake Bangweulu (The Field, London, ca. 1932).

28. The Luangwa National Parks: Astle, W.L.: South Luangwa National Park Map, Landscape & Vegetation (W.L. Astle, London 1989); Clarke, John E. & Loe, Ian D.: A Guide to the National Parks of Zambia (Anglo American Corp. CA, 1974); Carr, Norman: The White Impala (Collins 1969).

29. The Story of Munda Wanga: Shay, Reg: The Gardener of Chilanga (Reader's Digest, August 1966); New Look for Munda Wanga (Press statement, Zal Holdings, Lusaka 30 October 1987; K700 000 Raised for Zoo (Times of Zambia, 10 June 1987; ZPA Shrugs off Protests (Times of Zambia 9 August 1995).

30. The Vegetable Ivory Palm: Storrs, A.E.G.: Know Your Trees (Forest Dept, Ndola, 1979).

31. A Tale of Teak: Hobson, Dick: The Oldest Railway Engines (NR Journal, Vol.IV, p.488); Summers, Roger: Some Historic Railway Lines at Livingstone (NR Journal, Vol.2, No.5, p78); Storrs, A.E.G.: Know Your Trees (Forest Department, Ndola, 1979).

32. The Big Tree: The Wayside Tree (Horizon, magazine of the RST group, December 1959); Storrs, A.E.G.: Know Your Trees (Forest Department, Ndola, 1979).

33. The Nyika Plateau: Williamson, G.: The Orchids of South-Central Africa (Dent, London, 1977); Clarke, John E. & Loe, Ian D.: A Guide to the National Parks of Zambia (Anglo American Corp. CA, 1974).

34. The Copper Flower: Horizon, magazine of the RST group, January 1959.

35. Where the Copper Came From: Garlick, W.G.: How the Copperbelt Orebodies Were Formed (Horizon, magazine of the RST group, August 1959).

36. The First Miners: T.A. Rickard: Curious Methods Used by Katanga Natives in Mining & Smelting Copper (Engineering & Mining Journal, January 8 1927); Clark, J. Desmond: Pre-European Copper Working in South Central Africa (South African Mining & Engineering Journal, 21 June 1957); Bison, M.: Prehistoric Archaeology of the North-Western Province of Zambia (PhD thesis at ZCCM Central Technical Library, Kitwe); Horizon, magazine of the RST group, May 1959.

37. The Story of Kabwe Mine: Heath, K.C.G.: Mining & Metallurgical Operations at Rhodesia Broken Hill (Tr. Inst. Mining & Metallurgy, Vol. 70, Part 12, 1960–61); Clark, J. Desmond: The Prehistory of Africa (Thames & Hudson, 1970); Clark, J. Desmond: The Prehistory of Southern Africa (Penguin, 1959); Bancroft, J.A.: Mining in Northern Rhodesia (BSA Company, 1961); Davey, Thomas G.: General Report to the Northern Copper (BSA) Co. Ltd (London 1902); Horizon, magazine of the RST group, December 1963.

38. The Tale of the Roan Antelope: Coleman, Francis L.: The Northern Rhodesia Copperbelt 1899–1962 (Manchester UP, 1971); Prain, Ronald L.: Selected Papers 1958–60, p.133

(Batsford, London, 1961, for RST); Tapson, Winifred: Old Timer (Howard Timmins, Cape Town, ca. 1957).

39. Sanguni, the Luanshya Snake: Watson, Sir Malcolm: African Highway (John Murray, London, 1953; Stephenson, J.E.: The Luanshya Snake (NR Journal, Vol. 6, p13); Spearpoint, F.: The African Native & the Rhodesian Copper Mines (Supp. to Journal of the Royal Africa Society, Vol. XXXVI, No.CXLIV, 1937); Irwin, D.D.: Early Days on the Copperbelt (NR Journal, Vol. 6 p113).

40. The Prince & the Power Station: Heath, K.C.G.: Mining & Metallurgical Operations at Rhodesia Broken Hill (tr. Inst Mining & Metallurgy Vol. 70, Part 12, 1960–61); RCM Ltd: Zambia's Mining Industry – the First 50 Years (Ndola, 1978); Price, G. Ward: Through South Africa with the Prince (Gill Publishing, London, 1926).

41. How We Lost Katanga: Moloney, Joseph A.: With Captain Stairs to Katanga (Sampson Low, London, 1893); Johnston, H.H.: British Central Africa (Methuen, London, 1897); Rotberg, Robert I.: The Founder (Oxford UP, 1988).

42. The Mine that Nearly Died: Mufulira Mine Disaster: Final Report of the Commission of Inquiry (Government Printer, Lusaka, 1971); Mufulira – the Mine that Nearly Died (Zimco quarterly magazine Enterprise No.3 1975).

43. Burning the Bush: Austen, A.L.: Wood Fuel in Northern Rhodesia (Mining Magazine, October 1952); Duff, C.E.: Bashing the Bush (NR Journal Vol.2, No.1, p.61); Anon: Kariba & the Copperbelt (Horizon, magazine of the RST group, March 1959 p.12); Anon. ms: A Brief History of the Copperbelt Power Co. Ltd (CPC 1985).

44. Dr. Livingstone Died Here: Jeal, Tim: Livingstone (Heinemann, London, 1973); Johnson, Harry: Night & Morning in Dark Africa (London Missionary Society ca. 1902); Clark, J. Desmond: David Livingstone Memorial at Chitambo's (NR Journal, Vol 1, No.1 p.24); Simpson, Donald: Dark Companions (Paul Elek, London, 1975).

45. The Last Shots of World War I: Miller, Charles: Battle for the Bundu (Macdonald, London, 1974); Brelsford, W.V.: Story of the Northern Rhodesia Regiment (Government Printer, Lusaka, 1954); Hobson, R.H.: Rubber (Occasional Paper No.13, Rhodes-Livingstone Museum, 1960); Gore-Browne, Sir Stewart: The Chambeshi Memorial (NR Journal, Vol.2 No.5); Pullon, E.C. (ed): A Bush Telegraph (E.C. Pullon, Durban, 1994); ms. Copies of despatches from H. Croad, 1918).

46. The Statue of Chief Mukobela: Ferris, N.S. (ed): Know Your Rhodesia & Know Nyasaland (Rhodesian Printing & Publishing Co., Salisbury, 1956); Smith, Edwin W., & Dale, Andrew M.: The Ila-Speaking Peoples of Northern Rhodesia (Macmillan, London, 1920); Read, J. Gordon: The Ila Buffalo Drive, 1933 (NR Journal Vol.1, No.4 p.62).

47. Launching the Good News: Moir, Fred: After Livingstone (Hodder & Stoughton, London, ca. 1922); Hainsworth, F.C.: The Launching of the Good News (NR Journal, Vol. 1, No.3 p.17); Horne, C. Silvester: The Story of the LMS 1795–1895 (LMS, London, 1894); Clay, G.C.R., letter (NR Journal, Vol. 11, No.5, p.75).

48. The Oldest Church in Zambia: Brelsford, W.V., Phillipson, D.W., & Hickman, A.S.: Niamkolo Church (NR Journal, Vol.6, p24).

49. The Old Slave Tree: Clark, Dr. J. Desmond: letter to author, 18 August 1957.

50. Remembering Dag Hammarskjold: Welensky, Sir Roy: Welensky's 4000 Days (Collins, London, 1964); Hempstone, Smith: Katanga Report (Faber, London, 1962); Paynter, Marta (Times of Zambia, 14 September 1991); National Mirror, Lusaka, 14–20 September 1992, p.6.

51. Chitukutuku: NR Journal Vol. 3 p548–559; Vol. 4 p197, p610; Hobson, R.H.: Rubber (Occasional Paper No.13, Rhodes-Livingstone Museum, 1960).

52. The Cenotaph: Ferris, N.S. (ed): Know Your Rhodesia & Know Nyasaland (Rhodesian Printing & Publishing Co., Salisbury, 1956, p.101).

53. Nine Dead Soldiers: Anon: Author's Narrowest Escape (Times of

Zambia, 5 October 1993); correspondence with Charles Stacey, Ndola; S.J. Griffin, Miss M.C. Forrest and Eric C. Pullon, Amanzimtoti, South Africa; Lt-Col. Harry Klein, Johannesburg; Mrs. Heather Hunt, Kabwe; South African Air Force, Accidents Investigation Branch; South Africa Agency of the Commonwealth War Graves Commission; Klein, Harry: Land of the Silver Mist (Timmins, Cape Town, ca. 1952).

54. The Chirundu Fossil Forest: Ferris, N.S. (ed): Know Your Rhodesia & Know Nyasaland (Rhodesian Printing & Publishing Co., Salisbury, 1956, p.222).

55. The Sacred Burial Grove: Roberts, Andrew D.: A History of the Bemba (Longman, London, 1973); Hobson, Dick: Food & Good Fellowship (Lusaka Lunch Club, 1983).

56. Kanamakampanga: Doke, C.M.: Trekking in South Central Africa (South African Baptist Historical Society, 1975).

57. Chiengi Charlie: Alexander, Thomas: The Fate of 'Chiengi Charlie', Man-eater (NR Journal, Vol. 5, p.611).

58. An Aerial Adventure: Hobson, Dick: Food & Good Fellowship (Lusaka Lunch Club, 1983); Gale, W.D.: The Rhodesian Press (Rhodesian Printing & Publishing Co., Salisbury, 1962); The Eagle (Diocese of Northern Rhodesia, March 1953).

59. Beer: Doke, C.M.: The Lambas of Northern Rhodesia (Harrap, London, 1931); Smith, Edwin W., & Dale, Andrew: The Ila-Speaking People of Northern Rhodesia (Macmillan, London, 1920); Chicken, R.T.: A Report on an Inquiry into the Prevalence of Illegal Brewing, etc (Government Printer, Lusaka, 1948); Moore, R.J.B.: These African Copper Miners (Livingstone Press, London, 1948); Davis, J. Merle: Modern Industry & the African (Macmillan, London, 1933; 2nd ed. Frank Cass, London 1967); Storrs, A.E.G.: Know Your Trees (Forest Department, Ndola, 1979); Vasse, William: Three Years' Sport in Mozambique (Pitman, London, 1909); Powdermaker, Hortense: Copper Town (Harper & Rowe, New York, 1962).

60. Mwanambinyi's Hole: Prins, Gwyn: The Hidden Hippopotamus (Cambridge UP, 1980); Liswaniso, Mufalo: The Legend of Mwanambinyi (Horizon, magazine of the RST group, May 1967).

61. The Legend of the Kongamato: Melland, F.H.: In Witch-Bound Africa (Seeley, Service & Co., London 1923); NR Journal, Vol.4 p.411, Vol.5 p.86.

62. The Hare, the Elephant & the Hippopotamus: Melland, Frank: Elephants in Africa (Country Life, London, 1938).

63. Chisolo, the Great African Game: Tracey, H.T.: The Rules of the Native Game Tsoro (Native Affairs Department Annual, Salisbury, 1931, p33)

64. Lundazi Castle: Hobson, Dick: Notes of an interview with E.L. Button, MBE, ca. 1964.

65. The Cathedral of the Holy Cross: Diocesan brochure, 1962; correspondence with R.E.G. Hope, Ian Reeler, Canon J.E. Houghton, Canon A. Webster-Smith; Horizon, magazine of the RST group, January 1963.

66. The Victoria Falls Bridge: Pauling, George: The Chronicles of a Contractor (Constable, London, 1926); Clark, J. Desmond (ed): The Victoria Falls Handbook (Commission for the Preservation of Natural & Historical Monuments & Relics, Livingstone, 1952); Beira & Mashonaland & Rhodesia Railways: Guide to Rhodesia (2nd ed. Waterlow, London 1924); Davison, Arthur: Subscriber No.1 (NR Journal, Vol.1, No. 5, p.46); White, Beverley: The Trailmakers (Illustrated Life Rhodesia, 31 May 1973); Rotberg, Robert I.: The Founder (Oxford UP, 1988).

67. Tazara, the Freedom Railway: Hall, Richard, & Peyman, Hugh: The Great Uhuru Railway (Gollancz 1977); Tanzania-Zambia Railway Authority: Ten Years of Tazara Operations (Contact Advertising Ltd, Lusaka, 1986); Arnold, Stuart: Ten Years on the Tracks (African Technical Review, London, December 1986).

68. Cairo Road: Sampson, Richard: So This Was Lusaakas (Multimedia Publications, Lusaka, 2nd ed. 1971); Williams, Geoffrey J.(ed): Lusaka & its Environs (Zambia Geographical Association Lusaka, 1986); Gilg, A. Cameron: Turn Left – the Riffs Have Risen (Royal Automobile Club, London, 1981); Wilson, E.M.: The Kelsey Expedition (NR Journal, Vol.4, p.546).

69. The House at Crocodile Lake: Rotberg, Robert I.: Black Heart (U. of California, 1977); NR Journal Vol.5 pp315, 624; Vol.2 No.4 p.39; Vol.5 p540; Vol 6 p235.

70. The Saucepan Radio: Franklin, H.: Report on the Development of Broadcasting to Africans in Central Africa (Government Printer, Lusaka, 1950); Franklin, Harry: The Flag-Wagger (Shepheard-Walwyn, London, 1974); Bradley, Kenneth: Once a District Officer (Weidenfeld & Nicolson, London, 1966); Fraenkel, Peter: Wayaleshi (Weidenfeld & Nicolson, London, 1959); Smyth, Rosaleen: Historical Journal of Film, Radio & Television, London, Vol.4, No.2, 1984).

71. The Livingstone Museum: Clark, J. Desmond: The Rhodes-Livingstone Museum (ms of article for The Times, London, 24 February 1953); Hudson, R.S.: Livingstone Memorial Museum Handbook (Government Printer, Lusaka, 1936); Brelsford, W.V.: Handbook of the David Livingstone Memorial Museum (Government Printer, Lusaka, 1938); Horizon, magazine of the RST group, October 1964; Sampson, Richard: They Came to Northern Rhodesia (Government Printer, Lusaka, 1956).

72. The Great North Road: Hobson, R.H.: Rubber (Occasional Paper No.13, Rhodes-Livingstone Museum, 1960); Lane-Poole, E.H: The Great North Road (NR Journal, Vol.4, p.385); Horizon, magazine of the RST group, August, September 1966.

73. The Great East Road: Pauling, George: The Chronicles of a Contractor (Constable, London, 1926); Brelsford, W.V. (ed): Handbook to the Federation of Rhodesia & Nyasaland (Cassell, London, 1960); Gelfand, M.: Northern Rhodesia in the Days of the Charter (Blackwood, Oxford, 1961); Hailey, Lord: An African Survey (Oxford UP, 1938); Ridley, N.C.R.: Early History of Road Transport in Northern Rhodesia (NR Journal, Vol.2, No.5); Gann, L.H.: A History of Northern Rhodesia (Chatto & Windus, 1964); Tapson, Winifred: Old Timer (Howard Timmins, Cape Town, ca. 1958); Brelsford, W.V.: The Story of the Northern Rhodesia Regiment (Government Printer, Lusaka, 1954); Horizon, magazine of the RST group, December 1965.

74. The University of Zambia: Coombe, Trevor: The Origins of Secondary Education in Zambia (African Social Research, University of Zambia, No.3, Manchester UP, 1967); Williams, Geoffrey J.: The Peugeot Guide to Lusaka (Zambia Geographical Association, Occasional Study No.12, Mission Press, Ndola, 1987); Clifford, Bill: The Needs of a Nation (Horizon, magazine of the RST group, April 1963); Charlton, Les: Zambia University (Horizon, November 1965); Mlenga, Kelvin: The University of Zambia (Horizon, October 1968); Mukupo, Titus B. (ed): Kaunda's Guidelines (TBM Publicity Enterprises, Lusaka, 1970).

75. The National Assembly: Horizon, magazine of the RST group, May 1967.

76. A Capital Move: Collins, John, in Williams, Geoffrey J. (ed): Lusaka & Its Environs (Zambia Geographical Assocation Handbook Series No.9, Lusaka 1986); Hobson, Dick: Show Time (Agricultural & Commercial Society of Zambia, 1979); Hobson, Dick: Food & Good Fellowship (Lusaka Lunch Club, 1983); Varian, H.F.: Some African Milestones (George Ronald, London, 1953).

77. King Lewanika of Bulozi: "Pula": The Barotse People & Some of Their Customs (Native Affairs Department Annual, Salisbury, 1926); Clay, Gervas: Your Friend, Lewanika (Robins Series No.7, Chatto & Windus, 1968); Roberts, Andrew: A History of Zambia (Africana Publishing Co., New York, 1979); Prins, Gwyn: The Hidden Hippopotamus (Cambridge UP, 1980); Rotberg, Robert I.: Christian Missionaries & the creation of Northern Rhodesia (Princeton UP, 1965); Caplan, Gerald L.: The Elites of Barotseland (C. Hurst & Co., 1970); Bradley, Kenneth: Statesmen: Coryndon & Lewanika in North-Western Rhodesia (NR Journal, Vol.4, p.127).

78. The White Chief of the Bemba: Rotberg, Robert L.: Christian Missionaries & the Creation of Northern Rhodesia (Princeton UP, 1965); Roberts, Andrew D.: A History of the Bemba (Longman, London, 1973); Howell, Fr. A.E.: Bishop-King of the Brigands (Samuel Walker, London, 1944).

79. Butala bwa Maka's Museum: Corbeil, Fr. J.J.: Mbusa: Sacred Emblems of the Bemba (Moto Moto Museum, Mbala:

Ethnographica Publishers, London, 1982); Letter to author, National Museums of Zambia, 7 January 1991).

80. The Little Giant: Oliver, Roland: Sir Harry Johnston & the Scramble for Africa (Chatto & Windus, London, 1957); Harry Johnston – the Little Giant (Horizon, magazine of the RST group, March 1963); Willie Lamond (Horizon, November 1965).

81. Bwana Changa Changa: Brelsford, W.V.: Generation of Men (Stuart Manning, Bulawayo, 1965); Brelsford, W.V.: Harrison Clark – King of Northern Rhodesia (NR Journal, Vol.2, No.4, p.13); Earl-Spurr, N.O.: John Harrison Clark (NR Journal, Vol.2, No.6, p.91); Bentley, A.M.: Harrison Clark (NR Journal, Vol.2, No.6, p.93); Jordan, E. Knowles: Feira in 1919–20 (NR Journal, Vol.4, p.63).

82. Chirupula: Stephenson, J.E.: Chirupula's Tale (Geoffrey Bles, London, 1937); Rukavina, Kathaleen Stevens: Jungle Pathfinder (Hutchinson, London, 1951); Hobson, Dick: Chirupula Stephenson (Horizon, magazine of the RST group, May 1961); Chirupula, the Legend Grows, the Traces Fade (Horizon, May 1965); Cavill, John: Funeral of Chirupula Stephenson (NR Journal, Vol.3, p459).

83. Yengwe & the Hospital: Davison, Arthur: Subscriber No.1 (NR Journal, Vol.1, No.5, p.46); Brelsford, W.V.: Generation of Men (Stuart Manning, Salisbury, 1965); Work on One of Federation's Biggest Hospitals Begins Next Year (Northern News, Ndola, 30 November 1956).

84. Rhodes's Young Men: Roberts, Brian: Cecil Rhodes (Hamish Hamilton, London, 1987); Gelfand, M.: Northern Rhodesia in the days of the Charter (Blackwell, Oxford, 1961); Brelsford, W.V.: Generation of Men (Stuart Manning, Salisbury, 1965); Horizon, magazine of the RST group, February 1962; Gann, L.H.: The Birth of a Plural Society (Manchester UP, 1958); Le Soeur, Gordon: Cecil Rhodes (John Murray, London, 1913).

85. The Gentleman Adventurer: Brelsford, W.V.: Generation of Men (Stuart Manning, Salisbury, 1965); Copeman, E.A.: George Grey (NR Journal, Vol.2, No. 3, p.23); Sharp, R.R.: Early Days in Katanga (Rhodesian Printers, Bulawayo, 1956); Thornhill, J.B.: Adventures in Africa (John Murray, London, 1915); Bulawayo Chronicle, 28 May,1916 (in NR Journal, Vol.3 p.146); Horizon, magazine of the RST group, July 1962.

86. Sikorski's Tourists: Antkiewicz, Henry J.: Sikorski's Tourists in Tropical Africa: Administring World War II Polish Refugees in Northern Rhodesia. (Unpublished ms, copyright Dr. Henry J. Antkiewicz, East Tennessee State University).

Epilogue: Lammond, Rev. W.: Fifty Years in Central Africa (NR Journal, Vol.1, No.3, p.3); Brelsford, W.V.: The Story of the Northern Rhodesia Regiment (Government Printer, Lusaka, 1954); Mason, Philip: The Birth of a Dilemma (OUP 1958).

INDEX

223